# THE INFORMATION SOCIETY AND THE WELFARE STATE

# THE INFORMATION SOCIETY AND THE WELFARE STATE

*The Finnish Model*

**Manuel Castells**
**Pekka Himanen**

OXFORD
UNIVERSITY PRESS

# OXFORD

UNIVERSITY PRESS

Great Clarendon Street, Oxford OX2 6DP

Oxford University Press is a department of the University of Oxford.
It furthers the University's objective of excellence in research, scholarship,
and education by publishing worldwide in

Oxford New York

Auckland Bangkok Buenos Aires Cape Town Chennai
Dar es Salaam Delhi Hong Kong Istanbul Karachi Kolkata
Kuala Lumpur Madrid Melbourne Mexico City Mumbai Nairobi
São Paulo Shanghai Taipei Tokyo Toronto

Oxford is a registered trade mark of Oxford University Press
in the UK and in certain other countries

Published in the United States
by Oxford University Press Inc., New York

© ⬥ SITRƎ Helsinki, 2002

Sitra's publication series, publication no. 250,
ISSN 0785–8388 (Sitra)
Sitra – the Finnish National Fund for Research and Development

The moral rights of the authors have been asserted
Database right Oxford University Press (maker)

First published 2002

British Library Cataloguing in Publication Data
Data available

Library of Congress Cataloging in Publication Data
Data available

ISBN 0–19–925699–3

10 9 8 7 6 5 4 3 2 1

Typeset by Newgen Imaging Systems (P) Ltd., Chennai, India
Printed in Great Britain
on acid-free paper by
Biddles Ltd., Guildford and King's Lynn

# Acknowledgments

This book about networked Finland has itself benefited from our interaction with a large network of generous people. We would especially like to thank our talented research assistants, Sampsa Hakulinen and Anna Uusitalo, with whom we built many of the empirical files upon which this book is based. We would also like to thank Päivi Keinänen and Pekka Tossavainen at Statistics Finland, and Matthew Zook of the University of California at Berkeley, who helped us in building the empirical basis for our analysis of the flexible work and the spatial distribution of the Internet in Finland.

Antti Hautamäki and others at Sitra, the National Fund for Research and Development, have been generous both in their intellectual interaction and in their material support for the research. We particularly appreciate the absolute independence under which we have been able to conduct our research following our usual academic standards. We are also grateful to Jerry Feldman of the University of California at Berkeley, Pekka Ylä-Anttila of Etla, the Research Institute of the Finnish Economy, Antti Kasvio, Director of the Information Society Research Center at Tampere University, and Martti Mäntylä and Jukka Kemppinen of the Helsinki Institute for Information Technology for their thoughtful comments. With gratitude, we remember the late Risto Johnson – the pioneer journalist of the Finnish information society – with whom we had the chance to have many illuminating conversations.

In our search for the Finnish model, we have been in discussion with literally dozens of other builders of the Finnish information society from political leaders, such as Prime Minister Esko Aho and Foreign Minister Erkki Tuomioja, and business leaders, such as Nokia's CEO Jorma Ollila and President Pekka Ala-Pietilä, to hackers like Linus

## Acknowledgments

Torvalds and citizen activists like Veli-Antti Savolainen. Unfortunately, networking with so many people means that it is impossible to express here the thanks due to everyone individually. However, although prolific networking has this kind of unfortunate downside, we hope that others have also felt that the joys of collaborative networking greatly outweigh its shortcomings.

Manuel Castells and Pekka Himanen
*Berkeley, California, July 2001*

# Contents

# List of Figures

# List of Figures

# List of Tables

# List of Maps

It is fair to say that Finland is a country that loves progress and gallops towards it through all possible paths. What it is still missing is the main thing: what they understand as progress.

Angel Ganivet, *Cartas Finlandesas*, 1905

Chapter 1

# INTRODUCTION
# The Finnish Information Society in a Global Context

We are living in a time characterized by the rise of the information society in its diverse reality. The foundation of this society is informationalism, which means that the defining activities in all realms of human practice are based on information technology, organized (globally) in information networks, and centered around information (symbol) processing.[1] Thus, the core of the informational economy is the information-technology based global network of financial markets, where investors constantly shift their capital between securities

---

[1] The theory was first presented by Manuel Castells in his trilogy *The Information Age: Economy, Society, and Culture* (1st edn, 1996; 2nd edn, 2000a) and, in a more formalized version, in "Materials for an Exploratory Theory of the Network Society" (2000b). An extensive theoretical and empirical justification of the theory is given in these works. For the concept of informationalism, see also Castells's "Informationalism and the Network Society" in Himanen (2001).

with the help of computer models able to analyze information at high speed in real time. Companies maximize their productivity, market value, and ultimately profits by organizing themselves as networks, by applying information technology and by creating products that are increasingly based on information (symbol) processing. These networks are built around business projects, and are usually formed by components belonging to different firms. Thus, networking transforms the internal organization of the firm, its relationship to consumers and suppliers, and its partnerships with other firms. The resulting organizational form is what we conceptualize as the "network enterprise." In this new system of production and management, the labor force operates in the network enterprise as a constantly transforming network of decision-making and task implementation. Thus, jobs require not only the capacity to use information technology and process information, but also the ability to learn: labor with self-programming capability is at the source of productivity and competitiveness. It follows from this that the production of self-programmable, high-quality labor in a given society is the most important factor of production to win a competitive advantage in the informational economy.

The rise of the "network society" (using the term under which we conceptualize what the media describe as the "information society") is associated in the business world with the development of the "new economy", which dominated the minds and investment portfolios of the late 1990s. Its icons are Silicon Valley and, to some extent, the emerging Asian economies, especially Singapore (largely because it is often thought to be the model that China would like to follow). But there are other processes of structural transformation toward informationalism that offer a sharp contrast in terms of institutional foundations and social consequences, while reaching similar results in terms of technological innovation, productivity growth, and economic competitiveness. Our argument is that the information society can exist, and indeed does exist, in a plurality of social and cultural models, in the same way that the industrial society developed in very different, and even antagonistic, models of modernity, for instance in the United States and the Soviet Union, as well as in Scandinavia or Japan.

As was the case with the industrial society, the information society does have some common structural features around the world: it is based on knowledge generation and information processing, with the help of micro-electronics based information technologies; it is organized in networks; and its core activities are networked on a global scale, working as a unit in real time thanks to the infrastructure of telecommunications and transportation. This socio-technical structure develops and expands on the basis of its superior performing capacity, by phasing out through competition the organizational forms from the industrial era that are based on vertical, less flexible forms of management and implementation, less able to globalize their operating models. Thus, in a sense, all societies evolve toward adopting the features characteristic of the information society, even if in most of the world this transformation affects only the dominant functions and processes that are connected to the global networks of wealth creation and information processing.

At the same time, however, what we observe is that the paths and outcomes of this transformation are extraordinarily diverse. To be sure, countries around the world become informational at different speeds and in sharply divergent degrees, according to their level of development. But there is something else: societies and economies can reach very similar levels of techno-organizational informationalism starting from different histories and cultures, using a variety of institutions, and reaching distinct forms of social organization. In sharp contrast with the one-dimensional views of many futurologists, the world is not about to be made of Silicon Valleys, or would-be Silicon Valleys. There is a common information technology, and a global economy, but in the midst of human diversity. There is no one model of information society, ultimately represented by the United States and California, that serves as the standard of modernity for the rest of the world. The significance of the Information Age is, precisely, that it is a global, diverse, multicultural reality.

Within this framework of analysis, our interest in Finland as an information society stems from three basic concerns. The first is to investigate the process by which Finland emerged as one of the most competitive economies and most technologically developed information societies in the world, while displaying social and institutional features that stand in clear contrast to the Silicon Valley model or, for that matter, the Asian experience. Second, because of the importance of the welfare state in Finland, we are interested in understanding its role in the development of the information society. Since the new economy is often associated in expert circles around the world with liberalization and disengagement from the public sector in society, we would like to answer the following question: is the welfare state a contributing force to the full development of informationalism? Or, rather, are we misled by an optical illusion, as the industrial society fades away slowly with the old system still in place, and while the information society emerges, but not yet fully fledged, from the dynamics of entrepreneurial networks in a liberalized and privatized institutional context? Research, not ideology, should be able to provide tentative answers to these fundamental questions, at the roots of public policy and business strategy. Last, but not least, the relationship between globalization and national identity is complex and often contradictory. The inability of global networks of information and wealth to respect the values of historically rooted identities has created a great deal of instability in the world, as the feeling of meaninglessness triggers potentially fundamentalist reactions. Yet, Finland displays, at the same time, a dynamic integration in the global economy, fully fledged membership of the European institutions, and a strong affirmation of its culture, unique language, and national identity. Indeed, we propose the hypothesis that it is this identity, which provides a key foundation for political legitimacy, that enables the role of the state in the building of the information society.

Let us present this argument – about the socially distinct, yet technologically and economically equally dynamic, Finnish model of the information society – in more empirical terms. International studies show that Finland is, on the technological-economic dimension, as advanced as Silicon Valley or Singapore. For example, when compared using the criteria of the UN Technology Achievement Index, these three models are as shown in Fig. 1.1. (See also the larger comparative Table 1.1.)

Compared by competitiveness – a measure of economic dynamism – the United States, Singapore, and Finland rank as the three most dynamic economies in the world, according to the International Institute for Management Development (IMD), the leading competitiveness analyst (Fig. 1.2).

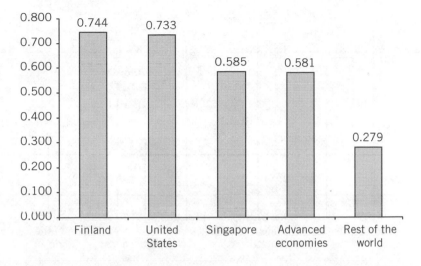

**Fig. 1.1 Technological development measured by the UN technology achievement index**

*Notes*: The index is based on four components: creation of technology (the number of patents granted per capita, the receipts of royalty and license fees from abroad per capita), diffusion of recent innovations (the diffusion of the Internet, exports of high- and medium-technology products as a share of all exports), diffusion of old innovations (telephones, electricity), and human skills (mean years of schooling, gross enrolment ratio of tertiary students enrolled in science, mathematics, and engineering).

By "advanced economies" we mean largely the same as the International Monetary Fund (IMF); that is, the Western economies (United States, Canada, Australia, New Zealand, Israel, United Kingdom, Ireland, Germany, France, Austria, Switzerland, Italy, Spain, Portugal, Greece, Norway, Denmark, Sweden, Finland) and the strongest Asian economies (Japan, Korea, Singapore – Hong Kong and Taiwan are not included here because they are not counted independently in all statistics). The aggregate figures have been calculated based on the UNDP (2001) as unweighted averages of the countries for which the technology achievement indices have been available (43 countries for the "rest of the world"). Here, as throughout the book, we have excluded from comparison countries with less than one million inhabitants, following the United Nations Population Fund statistical custom.

*Source*: UNDP (2001).

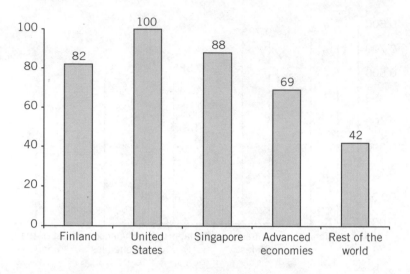

**Fig. 1.2 Economic development measured by the IMD competitiveness index**

*Notes*: The IMD's competitiveness figures are based on such economic criteria as GDP per capita, stock market capitalization, and productivity, as well as on a number of social criteria. Here the figure for the "rest of the world" represents a sample of 20 countries for which the data are available. These countries do not include any of the least developed economies in the world, so the figure represents rather the competitiveness of the most dynamic transitional/developing economies.

*Source*: IMD (2001).

The difference between the Finnish, Silicon Valley, and Singapore models becomes clear on the social level. The global trend is for the informational economy to connect to its network those who are valuable to it (and to add further value to them) but to disconnect those who are valueless (and thus further weaken their chance of acquiring any value). This results in increasing social injustice in the form of income inequality, polarization, and poverty. Using the ratio between the income of the richest 20 percent and the poorest 20 percent as a measure of social injustice, our areas are compared in Fig. 1.3.

In its extreme form, social injustice leads to social exclusion. Those individuals who are least valuable to the networks of informational

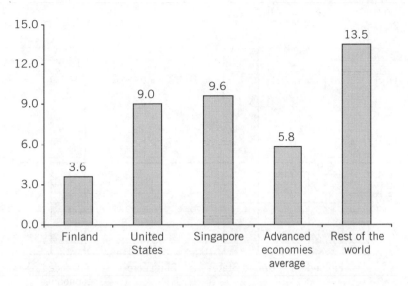

**Fig. 1.3  Social injustice measured by the ratio of the richest 20 percent to the poorest 20 percent**

*Notes*: Naturally, the higher the figure, the more unequal the country. The aggregate figures have been calculated as unweighted averages of the countries for which figures are available.

*Sources*: UNDP (2001), except for Singapore (UNDP, 1999) and New Zealand (UNDP, 2000).

capital – for example, because of educational, health, or social reasons – are left on their own, in a position from which it is very difficult for them to change their fate. The most violent way of survival is then to connect to the networks of global crime. Using functional illiteracy as a measure of the exclusion threat, our areas are shown in Fig. 1.4.

The difference in social injustice and exclusion between varying information society models can be seen especially well when we look at them through a longer time perspective. In the United States, the shift from an industrial to an information society, beginning in the 1970s, meant a reverse of the post-war trend. As can be seen in Fig. 1.5, until the 1970s social inequality was decreasing (measured by the Gini index) and exclusion was at a relatively low and stable level (measured by the incarceration rate). In the 1970s, both of these trends

7

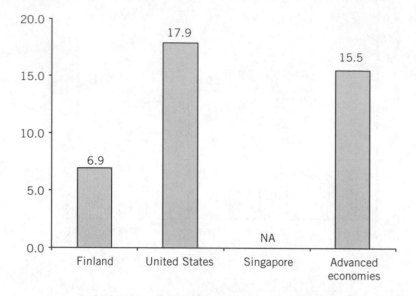

**Fig. 1.4 Social exclusion measured by functional illiteracy**

*Notes*: Functional illiteracy refers to, at most, Level 1 reading proficiency on the OECD PISA (Program for International Student Assessment) scale. The aggregate figures have been calculated as unweighted averages of the countries for which the figures are available.

*Source*: OECD (2001c).

turned to a rapid increase. In contrast, Finland's shift to the information society has been combined with a continued fall in, or, at least, a continued low level of social injustice and exclusion.

The rise of the network society has also generated a situation in which dominant values threaten other identities. There is a widespread feeling that the logic of the global networks of informational capitalism is not connected to cultural identity. This broken link between the predominant mode of development and specific identities questions the legitimacy of the development and creates resistance identities. At present, the information society is being challenged by social conflicts, ideological critiques, and resistance identities. By contrast, Finland is a country that stands out not only when we look at technological-economic development but especially when we

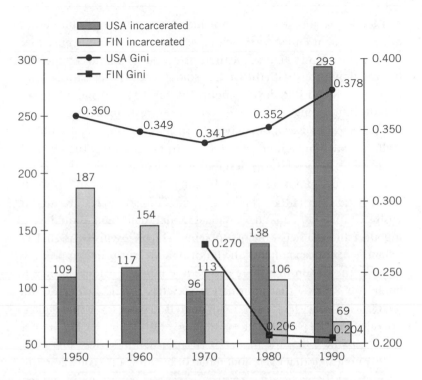

**Fig. 1.5 Social injustice and exclusion in the shift from an industrial to a network society in the United States and Finland, 1950–90**

*Notes*: In the Gini index, the value 1 means absolute inequality, in which one person gets everything and all others nothing, and the value 0 means absolute equality, in which everyone gets exactly the same. The above figure is primarily meant to show the trends of income inequality and incarceration. The figures for the United States are based on household gross income and the figures for Finland are based on per capita net income. However, because of the low level of income transfers, the United States gross and net income inequality figures are quite close to each other.

*Sources*: Gini figures are based on Deininger and Squire (1996). Incarceration figures for the United States are based on Cahalan (1986) and US Bureau of Justice Statistics (1992), and for Finland on von Hofer (1997).

consider social justice and legitimizing identity. The most interesting questions about Finland – which have much wider significance than for this one country alone – are then: "How does Finland combine the information society with the welfare state?" and, "What is the relation of Finnish identity to development?" What makes Finland internationally interesting is the fact that the Finnish model shows that technological and economic dynamism may be combined with the welfare state and legitimizing identity. In other words, the network society does not necessarily destabilize social order.

The purpose of our book is analytical, not normative. So it is worth stating explicitly that, by the expression "Finnish model," we do not wish to imply that Finland is an ideal model that others should try to imitate. Finland also has major problems, which we will discuss. In fact, what the real-life example of the Finnish model really does is precisely to reject the notion that there can be one model – earlier thought to be Silicon Valley – that information societies should follow. So, the political and policy lessons from our analytical work is not that Finland provides a better path to a more humane information society. Rather, the argument is that the model of an information society that every society builds, or that every individual or business firm contributes to, depends on the values that people, firms, and governments put forward. Within the same techno-economic paradigm (informationalism) there is considerable room for political choice based on values. And we will have to articulate sustainable values for the transformation of society and the economy, otherwise the contradictions of the social transition will trigger social explosions and violent opposition from a diversity of quarters. This is the message of our book, though we restrain ourselves from putting forward these values.

## The Finnish Model

There are several studies of the Silicon Valley and Singapore models,[2] but the Finnish model is known much more vaguely, often only on the level, to use the expression of the *Wired* cover story of 1999, that in

---

[2] For example, cf. Saxenian (1994, 1999) and Lee *et al.* (2000) for Silicon Valley and Castells *et al.* (1990) for Singapore.

Finland "the 21st century is in beta." It is therefore useful to briefly present some key facts about the Finnish case before moving to a more detailed analysis of its elements.

Finland's fame for being one of the most technologically advanced countries finds support from sources other than the UN Technology Achievement Index. Finland has held one of the top spots on the International Data Corporation's (IDC) Information Society Index since it was introduced in 1996.[3] Behind this index are facts such as, since the beginning of the 1990s Finland has led the field in Internet statistics, along with the United States, by the number of hosts per capita and the number of Internet users as a share of the population. For the same time period, Finland has also had the highest penetration rate of mobile phones (in 2001 about 80 percent of Finns had their own mobile phone). The most famous names in this strong technological development are Nokia, the world's biggest mobile telecommunications company (in 1999 Nokia became for a time the most valuable European company and the ninth most valuable in the world in terms of market capitalization), and Linux, the open-source operating system created by the Finn Linus Torvalds, which is considered to be the biggest challenger to the hegemony of Microsoft's operating system (Linux is already the leading web-server operating system).

By all the traditional criteria, the Finnish economy was very dynamic during the years 1996–2000, which is the latest for which data is available at the time of our writing. The annual growth of the Finnish GDP of 5.1 percent in this period was faster than that of the United States (4.3 percent), Japan (1.3 percent), and the average for the European Union (EU) (2.6 percent). This growth was driven by the information-technology (IT) cluster that includes Nokia, but is not limited to it. In the 1990s, labor productivity in the Finnish business sector grew by an annual average of 3.5 percent and in the manufacturing sector the growth was 7 percent, led by the telecommunications sector, which increased its productivity by an annual 25 percent. The value of stocks on the Helsinki Stock Exchange climbed by 894 percent in the five-year period between 1996 and the end of 2000. (It was even

---

[3] IDC (1996–2001); UNDP (2001).

11

higher in the peak year of 1999 and still remains, in the downturn of the economy, many times higher than at the beginning of this period.) As has been mentioned, in 2000 the IMD ranked Finland as the third most competitive economy in the world – the World Economic Forum (WEF) ranked it the most competitive.[4]

But the most distinctive feature of Finland is its combination of an information society and the welfare state. The Finnish welfare state includes totally free, high-quality, public education from kindergarten to the university (with one of the highest combined educational enrolment rates in the world), universal public health coverage (granted as a right based on citizenship), and a generous social system with universal retirement and unemployment insurance, which has made Finland a country with one of the smallest number of poor in the world. The welfare state is financed by high taxes, but high taxation proceeds with strong public support on the basis of the benefits most people receive from the welfare state.

In contrast to the crisis of legitimacy experienced by many governments throughout the world, which impairs their action, the Finnish state has been able to make bold policy decisions that paved the way for the new technological and economic dynamism of the 1990s. This has been achieved because the Finnish state has been seen as the bearer of Finnish identity. The non-conflictive relation between Finnish identity and the state has – in addition to the security provided by the welfare state – facilitated cooperation between the social actors involved in the restructuring process from the industrial to the informational economy.

Finnish history is an additional reason why we have chosen the Finnish model as the subject of our book. Finland can be distinguished from the other Nordic countries not only because it is now technologically and economically the most dynamic (and is the only one that is a world trendsetter in key technological fields such as mobile communications and open-source software) but also because, unlike the other Nordic countries, Finland was a relatively poor country not so long ago. Both the Finnish welfare state and the information society

---

[4] WEF (2000); IMD (2001).

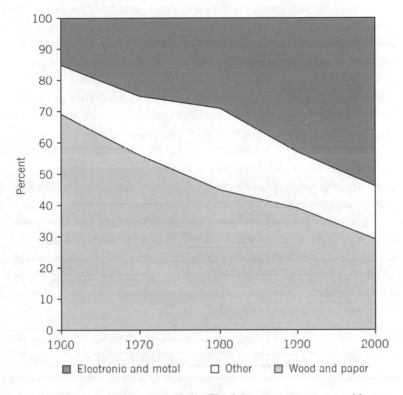

**Fig. 1.6** The transformation of the Finnish economy measured by export share, 1960–2000

*Source*: Etla, the Research Institute of the Finnish Economy.

have been built in the past couple of decades. Figure 1.6, showing the change in the structure of Finnish exports between 1960 and 2000, reflects the transformation well.

This gives the Finnish case a development perspective that makes it interesting for less advanced economies. The last big struggles in the Finnish transformation are as recent as the economic crisis of 1990–3, which threatened both the information society and the development of the welfare state. GDP contracted by 13 percent, and the unemployment rate rose from 3.5 percent to 17 percent in 1994. But, with the help of public policies, corporate restructuring, and individual innovators – relying on the welfare state (including the social contract between capital and labor) and legitimizing identity – the economy was turned around. In this process, Finland joined the EU (1995) and became an informational economy fully linked to global financial markets.

This book analyzes what happened and tries to define the main features that characterize the specificity of the Finnish model – as materials for further understanding Finland and the world we live in, not as a formal analytical model. In our study, it will also become clear that the Finnish model has many problems, one of which is unemployment that has not yet come down to less than 10 percent of the labor force. However, the main conclusion of our study is that Finland has been able to combine technological innovation and economic dynamism with the welfare state and legitimizing identity. In a time of increasing stress in the model of global development, it is worthwhile for all of us to reflect on the conditions and processes underlying the emergence of a socially sustainable network society, as represented by the recent experience of Finland.

**Table 1.1 A comparison of selected information society models**

| | Finland | United States | Singapore | Advanced economies |
|---|---|---|---|---|
| *Technology* | | | | |
| Infrastructure | | | | |
| 1 Internet hosts (per 1000 population) | 200 (1) | 179 (3) | 72 | 84 |
| 2 Mobile-phone subscriptions (per 1000 pop.) | 752 (1) | 401 (−3) | 583 | 589 |
| Production | | | | |
| 3 High-tech exports/total goods exports (%) | 27 | 32 (4) | 58 (1) | 21 |
| 4 e-Commerce (secure servers per 100 000 pop.) | 9.6 | 28.1 (1) | 14.6 (5) | 8.6 |
| Knowledge | | | | |
| 5 Internet users (%) | 46 | 49 (4) | n.a. | 33 |
| 6 Science, math, and engineering tertiary students (%) | 27 (1) | 14 | 24 (3) | 15 |
| *Economy* | | | | |
| National | | | | |
| 7 Competitiveness (index 0–100) | 83 (3) | 100 (1) | 88 (2) | 69 |
| 8 GDP per capita (US$) | 23 430 | 36 144 (3) | 22 949 | 22 666 |
| Business | | | | |
| 9 Productivity (manufacturing; index: 100 = USA) | 99 | 100 | n.a. | n.a. |
| 10 Stocks valuation growth, 1996–2000 (%) | 894 | 429 | n.a. | n.a. |

15

| | Col 1 | Col 2 | Col 3 | Col 4 |
|---|---|---|---|---|
| **Innovativeness** | | | | |
| 11 R&D investment/GDP (%) | 3.1 (3) | 2.6 | 1.9 | 2.0 |
| 12 Receipts of royalties and license fees (US$ per 1000 pop.) | 126 (5) | 130 (4) | 26 | 56 |
| *Welfare* | | | | |
| Education | | | | |
| 13 Primary, secondary, and tertiary enrolment (combined ratio) | 103 (4) | 95 | 75 (−1) | 94 |
| 14 Functional literacy (%) | 93 (2) | 82 | n.a. | 84 |
| Health | | | | |
| 15 Life expectancy at birth (years) | 77.2 | 76.5 (−5) | 77.1 | 78.0 |
| 16 Health insurance (%) | 100 | 82 | n.a. | n.a. |
| Welfare | | | | |
| 17 Richest 20% to poorest 20% (ratio) | 3.6 (3) | 9.0 (−3) | 9.6 (−2) | 5.8 |
| 18 People below the poverty line (%) | 3.8 (4) | 14.1 (−4) | n.a. | 10.6 |
| *Values* | | | | |
| Politics | | | | |
| 19 Freedom of the media (index: 0–100; 0 = free) | 14 (free) | 15 (free) | 68 (−1) (not free) | 19 (free) |
| 20 Gender empowerment measure (0–1000, 0 = unequal) | 783 (3) | 738 | 509 (−4) | 661 |

**Table 1.1  Continued**

|  | Finland | United States | Singapore | Advanced economies |
|---|---|---|---|---|
| **Civil society** |  |  |  |  |
| 21  Association membership | 1.8 | 1.1 | n.a. | n.a. |
| 22  Incarceration rate (per 100 000 pop.) | 62 (4) | 554 (−1) | 255 (−2) | 126 |
| **Globality** |  |  |  |  |
| 23  Foreigners or foreign-born / population (%) | 2.5 | 10.4 | n.a. | n.a. |
| 24  Environment: $CO_2$ emissions (per capita metric tons) | 10.9 | 20.1 (−2) | 23.4 (−1) | 10.4 |

*Note:* In Table 1.1, the dimensions have been chosen so that they can also be used to differentiate between various information society models. We can call a society an information society if it is strong in information technology (infrastructure, production, and knowledge). Of our selected countries, Finland, the United States, and Singapore qualify as advanced information societies. We can talk about a dynamic economy if it is internationally competitive, has productive business, and is innovative. Finland, the United States, and Singapore are all dynamic economies.

However, technology and economy are just part of the story. We can talk about an open society when it is open politically, as a civil society, and to global processes. The Western information societies differ from Singapore in being open societies, whereas Singapore's figures show it to be an authoritarian society. When we look at the welfare dimension, the United States is very much like Singapore, with sharp income inequality. The distinguishing feature of the Finnish information society, compared to both the United States and Singapore, is that it is also a generous welfare society. The difference is most clear in income distribution. In education and health, the United States and Finland have very similar aggregate figures for enrolment as an indicator of the general level of education, and for life expectancy as an indicator of the general level of health, but when the focus is on the excluded (functional illiteracy and health insurance) the difference is clear again. Finland ranks first in the world in all of these dimensions (the figures in parentheses indicate the position within the group of the 24 advanced economies – only the top five and bottom five positions are marked).

In sum, the table shows three very different economically and technologically dynamic models of the information society:

1 "the Silicon Valley Model" of a market-driven, open information society;

2 "the Singapore Model" of an authoritarian information society; and

3 "the Finnish Model" of an open, welfare information society.

Of course, these terms are general labels for types that contain more than just these countries or areas, although the above areas are arguably the most representative ones for each model.

*Sources:* 1, 3, 6, 12, 13, 15, 18, 20, 22, 24: UNDP (2001); 2, 5, 7, 8, 11: IMD (2001); 4: Netcraft (2001), figures are for January 2001; 9: Etla (2001); 10: Nasdaq (2001) and HEX (2001); 14: OECD (2001*c*); 16: Health Care Financing Review (1999); 17: World Bank (2000); 19: Freedom House (2001), 21: Putnam (1995) and Siisiäinen (1999), figures are for association memberships among people with only primary education in the mid-1990s; 23: Statistics Finland (2000) and US Census Bureau (2000). Population standardizations have been calculated based on UNFPA (2000) when the original data are in absolute figures. Figures for the advanced economies are averages of those countries for which data are available.

Chapter 2

# THE MOBILE VALLEY
## Nokia, Finland, and the Transformation of the Finnish Economy

*The Informational Economy*

On an economic level, in the shift from an industrial to a network society, we are witnessing a worldwide transformation from an industrial to an informational economy. This change permeates the key components of the economy from the financial markets through enterprises to the labor force.[1] At the core of the new informational economy are the informational financial markets that form a globally interconnected network, which is increasingly located in electronic networks, and in which investment requires the processing of increasingly complex

---

[1] Castells (2000a), here complemented with some additions based on Himanen (2001). The best empirical evidence for this change is presented by Held *et al.* (1999) for financial markets, Imai (1990) for enterprises, and Carnoy (2000) for labor.

information (symbols). The technological basis of the financial markets makes a qualitative difference because technology allows unprecedented speed in investment. Capital can also move globally in the markets, which can include more and more actors: as a result, in the currency markets alone more than the GDP of the United Kingdom (1.5 trillion dollars) is daily invested in more optimal destinations. And market values are determined in an increasingly complex way as a result of information (symbols) coming from more and more sources. Increasing speed, volume, and complexity multiply the volatility of the financial markets.

With financial markets at the heart of the informational economy, the market value of enterprises becomes the core criterion of their performance. However, this notion should not be confused with the "dotcom" vision of an economy whose center is e-commerce on the Net and in which none of the old laws of the economy apply. The empirical reality is not the "dotcom economy" but a much wider development of informational enterprises. In this form of enterprise, success is still based on profits in the long term. And the basis for economic growth is still ultimately productivity growth. The significant difference between the concepts of the dotcom and the informational economy has been well demonstrated in the development of market values during the economic downturn that began in 2000: those companies that make a profit have sustained their market value best. Nor was there economic growth in the late 1990s without productivity growth: it has been shown that, in the United States, labor productivity doubled between 1996 and 2000 (2.8 percent per year) compared with the preceding decade. In the IT sector, which led the growth in market value, labor productivity grew at a staggering 24 percent per year in the 1990s. Profits and productivity are still the foundation.

So, recent developments do not correspond to the vision of the dotcom economy. But nor can they be understood just on the basis of old economic theories. Market values have become the center of the economy in an unprecedented way and these market values are the sums of much more complex information (symbols) than before. The traditional "rational" economic factors, such as profits, revenues, and debt, continue to be decisive. Likewise, traditionally important political factors, such as stability, the regulatory environment, and the policy of the central bank, continue to be important in determining the total market. But other symbolic messages also have a new significance in an economy that is increasingly based on expectations characteristic of the culture of speed. In the fast economy, during good times, companies compete by promising that the future will arrive through them faster than through their competitors. In this situation, the feelings of expectation that affect investment are the fear of being late for the future and impatience about waiting for the future to arrive. But the fast economy also has equally speedy downturns: the theory of the informational economy does not include the dotcom belief in continuous growth; instead it describes the new nature of rapidly changing periods of growth and fall. In the fast economy, during bad times, the above feelings of expectation are replaced by two other feelings: disappointment that unrealistic future expectations were not realized and disbelief that there is a future at all. In this situation, companies compete by emphasizing how their competitors promise the future through their mediation, whereas they themselves focus on achieving results through the good old basic laws of the economy. Of course, in both phases of the fast economy the winners are those investors who understand the new role of expectation but do not succumb to either extreme in their own reaction. They look at things from a longer time perspective and do not let their feelings of expectation blind them from also seeing the traditional economic and political factors.

At the level of company structure, informational enterprises increase their productivity, profits, and market value by organizing themselves (globally) as networks, by applying information technology, and by focusing more and more on information (symbol) operation. This applies to the company's relationship with its employees, customers, and the financial markets. For employees: management, innovation, and production are organized as global networks, which can be coordinated with the help of computer networks. The result is an enterprise that consists internally of relatively autonomous units that network together for projects. Externally, the enterprises network with suppliers according to the varying needs of the projects. And enterprises also join forces with their size-equivalents to make the biggest efforts possible. The significance of symbol processing in production means that increasingly the product is symbol processing: the technology of symbol processing (information technology), the symbol processing itself (e.g., media products) or the symbolic experience that the product creates (e.g., when one buys a particular mobile phone, one also buys the experience that owning that phone creates). In innovation, the growing significance of symbol processing translates into the increasing role of innovation inside companies, and, in management, it translates into the increasing role that the company culture plays in success.

The relationship with customers is also networked: the informational enterprise's marketing, sales, and distribution are based on a network relationship that computer networks make possible. The sales are more and more on the Net, distribution is increasingly networked to external partners, and marketing gets exact information about consumer needs immediately based on sales. The significance of symbol processing means, from the customer's viewpoint, that brands become increasingly important. And, finally, the relationship with the financial markets has the same logic: in the informational financial markets, everything from funding to the growth of market value is increasingly based on the enterprise's ability to link to global electronic financial markets and to develop its symbolic level (image) consciously.

The informationalization of the financial markets and enterprises is connected to the rise of the informational labor force. First, employee relationships with the company are organized as a network. This means an increasing share of project-like work in the form of self-employment, temporary work (whether consulting or piecemeal jobs) and part-time work. Second, in most jobs some skills in information technology are needed. And third, within the labor force, the information (symbol) creators are increasingly the ones on whom economic growth relies.

## The Finnish IT Cluster

Worldwide, the driver of the above development has been the IT sector, although this development is in no way limited to it. Finnish development in the 1990s and the beginning of the third millennium is a good example of the pioneering role of the IT sector. Led by the IT sector, the total market value of Finnish companies grew by 894 percent from 1996–2000. The continued importance of profits has been seen well in the economic downturn that began in 2000: the market value of the dotcoms, whose value skyrocketed in the late 1990s despite their enormous losses, has plummeted equally dramatically; whereas the market value of Nokia, which continues to make big profits even in the downturn, has sustained its level better than its competitors. And, in Finland too, the ultimate basis for the economic growth of the 1990s was increased productivity. Since 1992, Finnish labor productivity has increased by 3.5 percent per year in the business sector, by 7 percent in the manufacturing sector, by 15 percent in the electro-technical sector, and by 25 percent in the telecommunications industry.[2]

The Finnish informational economy is based on its strong role as a producer of information technology. The IT cluster has become the most dynamic and competitive export sector.[3] As of 2000, the cluster, which employed only about 3–4 percent of the total labor force, accounted for one third of total exports and now accounts for about 45 percent of the Finnish GDP. The export share of IT production was over 60 percent, with 85 percent of total IT equipment manufacture exported. In fact, these figures put Finland on top of the world in terms of export sector specialization in telecommunications equipment and high-technology trade surplus (high-technology exports/ imports ratio).[4]

Even though Nokia is the core of the Finnish IT cluster and has shaped it into a "Mobile Valley" with a special strength in wireless telecommunications, there is more to Finland than Nokia (see Table 2.1). Nokia has some 300 suppliers in Finland, but the entire

[2] The data for this chapter have been obtained from Etla, the Research Institute of the Finnish Economy. See also Ali-Yrkkö *et al.* (2000), Paija (2000, 2001) and Ali-Yrkkö (2001).

[3] In this chapter, the "information-technology cluster" refers to information and communications technology manufacturing and information technology and telecom services.

[4] For international comparisons of information-technology specialization, see OECD (2000, 2001*a*).

**Table 2.1 Some Finnish IT cluster firms in 1999**

| Firm | Line of business | Sales (mEUR) | Personnel |
|---|---|---|---|
| *Infrastructure and terminals* | | | |
| Nokia Oyj[*] | Mobile phones and network systems | 30 376 | 58 708 |
| Tellabs Inc.[*] (ex. Martis Oy) (USA) | Network access and transfer systems | 3640 | 8643 |
| Teleste Oyj[*] | Access networks | 92 | 562 |
| Benefon Oyj | Mobile phones | 59 | 377 |
| Electrobit Oy[*] | Network equipment | 37 | 550 |
| Nemo Technologies Oy | Network measurement tools | n.a. | 40 |
| *Operation* | | | |
| Sonera Oyj[*] | Telecom and mobile operator | 2057 | 10 305 |
| Elisa Communications Oyj[*] | Telecom operator | 1244 | 6161 |
| Radiolinja Oyj | Mobile operator | 614 | 1058 |
| Jippii Group Oy | Internet service provider | 35 | 387 |
| *Components/contract manuf.* | | | |
| Elcoteq Network Oyj[*] | Electronic manufacturing services | 2214 | 9630 |
| Perlos Oyj[*] | Mobile phone enclosures | 452 | 3503 |
| NK Cables Oy (acquirer: Draka Holding, NL) | Communications cables | 286 | 800 |

| | | | |
|---|---|---|---|
| Flextronics Finland (ex. Kyrel EMS Oy) (USA) | Electronic manufacturing services | 253 | 532 |
| Aspocomp Oyj* | Printed circuit boards | 240 | 2007 |
| JOT Automation Group Oyj* | Industry automation | 140 | 746 |
| PKC Group Oyj* | Data transfer systems | 129 | 730 |
| Filtronic LK Oy (ex. LK-Products Oy) (UK) | RF filters, access products, antennas | 90 | 883 |
| Salcomp Oy | Power supplies and battery charges | n.a. | 650 |
| Wecan Electronics Oyj* | Telecom network electronics | 47 | 457 |
| Savcor Coatings Oy | Enclosure coatings | 3 | 90 |
| *Applications software* | | | |
| TietoEnator Oyj* | Enabling solutions | 1120 | 9934 |
| Tecnomen Oyj* | Unified messaging solutions | 66 | 484 |
| Comptel Oyj | Mediation device solutions | 60 | 426 |
| Samlink Oy* | Electronic banking systems | 45 | 243 |
| F-Secure Oyj* | Secure network solutions | 41 | 399 |
| CCC Oy | 3D software | 34 | 400 |
| SSH Communications Security Oyj* | Secure network solutions | 16 | 130 |
| First Hop Oy | Mobile access applications | n.a. | n.a. |

**Table 2.1** Continued

| Firm | Line of business | Sales (mEUR) | Personnel |
|---|---|---|---|
| *Ict consultancy* | | | |
| Satama Interactive Oyj* | Internet consultancy | 30 | 414 |
| TJ Group Oyj* | Internet consultancy | 29 | 404 |
| *Digital content/packaging* | | | |
| Sanoma-WSOY Oyj* | Media house | 11 448 | 10 350 |
| eQ Online Oyj* | Mobile brokerage services | 17 | 173 |
| Iobox Group* (acquirer: | | | |
| Terra Mobile, SPA) | Mobile portal | n.a. | 200 |
| WOW-Verkkobrandit Oy | Digital newspaper | 0.20 | 70 |
| Springtoys Oy | Mobile entertainment/platforms | 0.17 | 40 |

*Source:* Paija (2001).

Finnish IT cluster includes more than 3000 companies. Even Nokia's suppliers are not only working for Nokia. Nokia's partner, Elcoteq Network, is the largest European electronic manufacturing service company, which also works for many other companies. In all, there are about 240 Finnish electronic manufacturing service companies, which are diversifying their customers.

Telecommunication operators, such as the recently privatized telecom company Sonera, and its competitor Elisa Communications, are innovating in mobile services.[5] In fact, operator services provide another Finnish field of specialization. For example, Comptel is a world leader in subscriber data-management solutions for operators.

Communications security is also an expanding software niche, exemplified by companies such as SSH Communication Security (encrypting IP connections, which is the backbone of the future mobile Internet) and F-Secure (offering anti-virus software). A growing legion of mobile communication start-ups, such as Iobox (mobile device tones and icons), Add2Phone (mobile advertising), and Springtoys/Codeon line (mobile games) are developing content services for mobile platforms.[6] Two major multimedia groups, SanomaWSOY and Alma Media, have been constituted by the mergers of several media companies. There are also many successful smaller multimedia companies, such as the computer game houses Remedy Entertainment and Housemarque. Further, a number of multinational companies, particularly Ericsson, Hewlett Packard, and Siemens, have set up shop in the promising mobile environment constituted in Finland during the 1990s.

Electronic banking is the most advanced example of the diffusion of information technology to other sectors. For example, the Finnish bank Merita (part of the Scandinavian Nordea Bank) has been a leader in Internet and mobile phone banking services for years using the Finnish software company Tieto as its partner (now part of the Finnish–Swedish TietoEnator). As of spring 2001, it had twice as many

---

[5] For the history of the operator side of the Finnish IT business, see Häikiö (1998) and Steinbock (2001).

[6] For background on Finnish IT start-up companies, see Aula and Oksanen (2000).

online transactions per month as the second biggest in the world, the Bank of America (6.9 million online transactions per month). Samlike is another important Finnish company developing electronic banking systems. In fact, financial services are the best example of how the informational mode is increasing productivity in sectors other than IT production. In 1995–9, labor productivity grew by 11.7 percent per year in financial intermediation and by 13.2 percent in activities related to financial intermediation (compared to 2.2 percent and −4.1 percent during 1989–95).[7]

## Nokia's New Way: Recurrent Renewal or Historical Discontinuity?

So the Finnish IT cluster is by no means only Nokia, though it would be true to say that Nokia was the main driver in its growth in the 1990s. This is the reason why it is necessary to analyze the rise of Nokia in more detail. As we will see, the story of the Nokia model mirrors that of Finland's own transformation from the industrial to the informational economy. The key is the new business model that Nokia created, which is now spreading more widely in the Finnish IT cluster.

Nokia is a global company of 60 000 people, divided into two main businesses: Nokia Mobile Phones (manufacturing mobile communication devices) and Nokia Networks (building mobile communication networks and offering related services). Both of them are also divided internally into changing businesses. The two main divisions are supported by Nokia Research Center and Nokia Ventures Organization. Nokia Mobile Phones comprises about three-quarters and Networks one-quarter of all sales, and they both have around 25 000 employees. Nokia has research and development in fifteen countries, production in ten countries, and sales to over 130 countries.[8]

But the public image of Nokia as a company whose key to success is its capability to renew itself obscures a substantial historical discontinuity. In 1992–5 Nokia took a sharp turn from its previous

---

[7] OECD.    [8] Nokia (2000a,b).

trajectory in product lines, corporate structure, and financial basis. The old Nokia had grown on the basis of a business model that led to its crisis, and almost led to its extinction in 1989–91. In fact, it was on the verge of being taken over by Ericsson.

For most of its history, Nokia grew as a conglomerate of three very different businesses, of which the first was started in the town of Nokia, named after the river running through it.[9] These three companies were: Nokia, a wood-pulp/papermill founded in 1865; Finnish Rubber Works, established in 1898; and Finnish Cable Works, begun in 1912. After World War I, Finnish Rubber Works bought the majority of shares in the other two companies, thus consolidating financial control over the future components of the group long before their final merger as the Nokia Group in 1966.

In the 1970s and 1980s, Nokia expanded its activity to a wide variety of businesses, particularly in the area of consumer electronics (especially television), while a small part of the group began the development of mobile phones and of digital telecommunication exchanges (see Chapter 3 for an analysis of this important phase). In the late 1980s, Nokia had eleven divisions producing everything from toilet paper, rubber boots, and car tires to cables, computers, and televisions. The business model was a conglomerate of separate activities, with little synergy from their inclusion within the same group. Management was based on the old, industrial-patron style: a hierarchical structure, with strong control from the top of the group over each of its components. And the group entered new markets by acquiring assets and expanding, rather than by reallocation of resources. It was growth on an extensive model of capital accumulation, close to the German–Swedish tradition of expanding by addition rather than by networking. And this business model demanded a tight control over the whole set of the group's diverse operations.

---

[9] For a general history of Nokia see Häikiö (2001), which is based on original documents. See also Mäkinen (1995); Bruun and Wallén (2000); and Steinbock (2001). For the history of the present Nokia's predecessor companies, see also Ekman (1929); Hoving (1948); von Bonsdorff (1965); Cronström and Ström (1965); and Kuisma (1996).

The conglomerate model and hierarchical management practices led to serious crises in Nokia throughout the 1980s, the time when Nokia forcefully entered the television business. Nokia's dominant personality during this expansion was Kari Kairamo, who was appointed as the CEO in 1977.[10] The company ran into severe financial and personnel relations problems and Kairamo committed suicide in 1988 (here, of course, it should be remembered that suicide is always a complex personal matter and not necessarily linked to professional difficulties). Earlier, in January 1988, Nokia also lost some of its key engineers, who had designed its first successful mobile phone (these engineers founded Nokia's competitor, Benefon, another Finnish mobile-phone company which is now specializing increasingly in mobile navigation solutions). This was not the typical Silicon Valley story of innovative spin-off, but a story of bitter personal conflict, and strongly opposite views.

The situation deteriorated in the post-Kairamo era. The conflicts between the new CEO, Simo Vuorilehto (from the forestry industry), and the President, Kalle Isokallio (son-in-law of the chairman of the Board), hampered management reaction capacity at the very time that Asian producers were making their onslaught into consumer electronics. During this period, Nokia had to cut its workforce from 44 000 to 22 000. The collapse of the Soviet Union in 1991 drastically reduced a market that was still important to Finnish companies. And, partly for this reason, the Finnish economy, which was still a major market base for the Nokia Group, went into a tail-spin. In December 1991, Vuorilehto was pushed into retirement and Isokallio was dismissed. The future of Nokia was most uncertain, and the sale of the company was seriously considered. Thus, writing in 1992, the story of Nokia would have been one of business failure: the failure of a business model (multi-industrial conglomerate, vertical structure, and finance based on loans from banks) that had bet on a mature market without much future growth potential (television).

In 1992, Jorma Olilla, the head of the then small Nokia Mobile Phones division from 1990, was appointed as the CEO to manage the company out of the crisis. He dismissed the executives who

---

[10] For the role of Kairamo, see Michelsen (1996); Saari (2000); and Otala (2001).

represented the old consumer electronics and industrial-patron management style, and brought into the top management a group of like-minded professionals of his own generation (all in their thirties at the time). Ollila and his new management group completely transformed Nokia. They built on the expertise that Nokia had acquired in mobile communication in a long historical process (see Chapter 3), but made this expertise relevant in a new way by transforming the structure and focus of Nokia.

There has been enough of a personality cult around Ollila so there is no need to indulge it further. He is clearly an exceptional business innovator, and personalities do play a role in business success and failure. But what is analytically significant is to determine what Nokia did, under its new management, that reversed the fate of the company, and, with it, the structure of the whole Finnish economy. In a nutshell, Nokia transformed itself from an industrial to an informational company. Three new elements of the new business model were especially critical for the successful transformation of Nokia: a new product and industrial structure; a fundamental change in financial structure; and an innovative network enterprise model.[11]

Ollila expressed Nokia's statement of intent in 1992 as: "telecom oriented, global, focused, and value-added." In line with this strategy, Nokia decided to sell off most of its businesses and started to emphasize one product: mobile communication in its diverse and evolving forms. Here, Nokia acted both with a strategic vision about a digital mobile world and because it had little choice. Nokia had to finance an attempt to reverse its fall by trying to succeed in a selected field. So Nokia divested itself of all its businesses except mobile phones and telecommunications networks as soon as it could, and thus anticipated the evolution of technology and society toward ubiquitous communication, and, down the line, the ubiquitous Internet.

Nokia's new product, however, was not just based on engineering but also on social innovation. Nokia understood earlier than its competitors that the mobile phone is not just a technical device for a

---

[11] For earlier analyses of Nokia, see Tuomi (1999) and Steinbock (2001). In our analysis, we have also benefited from discussions with Nokia CEO Jorma Ollila, President Pekka Ala-Pietilä, Mobile Phones President Matti Alahuhta, Networks Vice President J. T. Bergqvist, and Nokia Strategy Manager Mikko Kosonen.

narrow business user group but a device for people as a whole, and that user-friendliness and design are a major part of its value. Nokia's breakthrough came with its stylish and easy-to-use mobile phones from 1992 onwards. Thus, Nokia understood early the significance of the symbolic experience as a source of value,[12] something that was reflected in 2000 by Interbrand's listing of Nokia as the fifth most valuable brand in the world. This and Nokia's ethos as a strongly customer-driven company are important factors in explaining why it could overtake both Motorola and Ericsson, both of which were much bigger than Nokia.[13]

Nokia also made another change that was fundamental to its later success: it transformed its financial structure. Before Ollila's time, Nokia had a very limiting financial structure, based on its income or debt to one of the two major Finnish banking groups. (While Nokia was, exceptionally, owned by both major Finnish banking groups, which gave it more independence than if it had been under the control of only one banking group as most Finnish companies were, this financial structure also jammed its decision-making because of the mutual power play of the banks.) It should be added that, while Finnish financial markets remained regulated, Nokia was stuck with its conglomerate model to ensure a constant cash flow to finance its new operations. It was only after the freeing of controls on capital movements from the end of the 1980s – including bond and equity – that it was possible for Nokia to obtain enough capital without giving up control to the banks.

In 1994, Nokia was listed on the New York Stock Exchange. And, in 1997, Nokia eliminated the traditional system of two kinds of shares with different voting rights. By doing so, it opened up to investors from around the world and gradually became one of the world's most valuable companies in market capitalization. This is in sharp contrast to its Swedish competitor, Ericsson, which is still controlled by family ownership through shares of the A/B system.

There are several reasons why this was so important. In the informational economy, the ability of management to react to a market

---

[12] For the concept of the "experience economy", see Pine and Gilmore (1999).
[13] See Pulkkinen (1996, 1997); Pantzar and Ainamo (2001).

situation depends on its independence *vis-à-vis* the personal interests of a minority of shareholders. This independence is strengthened by a finance system that depends exclusively on market valuation. There is also considerable evidence to show that increased foreign ownership has a positive influence on the transformation of companies by making them focus on their core competence, and by increasing the global flow of research and development, and operation in the more competitive global environment encourages the growth of their market valuation and profitability. Since valuation in financial markets is the definitive benchmark of company performance in the informational economy, the transformation of Nokia's ownership structure can be considered as the foundation of the new business model.

## Nokia as a Network Enterprise

The third change was Nokia's new enterprise model. In the informational economy, process and organizational innovations are as important as product innovation.[14] As Nokia has been at least as innovative in its enterprise structure as the best-known examples of this new company form, Cisco Systems and Dell, it is worth while to analyze this model in more detail. Further, this "Nokia model" is gradually radiating from Nokia to the rest of the Finnish IT sector and to other global companies.

It should be remembered that Nokia did not become a world market leader by always being a first-comer in the mobile phone market:[15] Nokia outperformed its competitors by way of its operation. Nokia began the transformation of its enterprise structure simultaneously with the development of its first mobile phone successes in 1992. The company decided that product, process, and organizational innovation must go hand in hand. The resulting model included strong networking with subcontractors and clients (the mobile phone dealers and the network buyers) at all levels. Since then, one of the keys to Nokia's

---

[14] For the significance of combining the use of information technology and organizational innovation, see Brynjolfsson (1997). For the relevance of process innovation, see Hammer and Champy (1993).     [15] Pulkkinen (1997).

performance has been its efficient logistics, which is based on the more transparent sharing of information with its partners than is done by its competitors. However, in the Nokia context, logistics does not just refer to the old, industrial idea of having the right number of products in the right place at the right time (although this just-in-time business practice remains important). It includes, as well, the rapid sharing of information about consumer needs and an immediate reflection of this information in innovation strategies and in the direction of production. Gradually, Nokia has moved this information-sharing more and more to electronic networks. A significant part of information exchange, sales, and support takes place through electronic networks.[16]

So, what is often referred to as Nokia's "efficient logistics" conceals a much broader network enterprise concept. The following sequential analysis of its key elements should not be understood as suggesting a linear process, starting from production, innovation, and management and ending with marketing, sales, and distribution. The model should rather be seen as a network of constant interaction: in fact, Nokia's strength has been precisely its holistic way of thinking. Also, because Nokia's organizational innovation is continuous, the following analysis focuses on its more permanent features.

*Production*

One-third of Nokia's employees are in production, but Nokia adds both flexibility and knowledge-sharing to its structure – two elements that are important for acting more dynamically in the fast economy – by networking part of its production. However, this is not the "outsourcing" of the industrial age – the using of subcontractors, selected through price competition, and limited to just getting the goods or services – but a deeper partnership in which operations are developed together, information is shared transparently, and the price efficiency is evaluated from a longer perspective. Nokia's production is located in a worldwide network, based on the quality and flexibility of labor and on political considerations (e.g., in China a local presence is central for business opportunities). As mentioned above, in Finland alone, Nokia has a network of some 300 partners. Nokia does not try

---

[16] It is also an indication of Nokia's efficient network that its IT costs are 3 percent of sales, below those of other leaders in the industry.

to do everything itself but it leverages the core competence of others. For example, it is the only major telecommunications manufacturing company that does not have its own component production (e.g., semiconductors). This allows Nokia to be less vulnerable to technology innovation outside itself. On the other hand, it makes good management of the network of subcontractors and component manufacturers very critical – something in which Nokia has succeeded as it suffers less from shortages than its competitors.

*Innovation*

Nokia's innovation or research and development expenditures are about 9 percent of net sales, and one-third of its employees are in research and development (divided between the corporate Research Center and the research and development of the business units, Nokia Mobile Phones, Nokia Networks, and Nokia Ventures Organization).[17] The share of sales spent on research and development is an indicator of the company's innovative capacity, but not a sufficient one. On mere figures, Ericsson and Motorola invest more than Nokia, although Nokia invests more than its Asian competitors such as NEC and Samsung. What matters at least as much as the amount spent is the nature of the research and development, and its network links to research and development in universities and other companies. Nokia's internal evaluation criterion for research and development is based on results, not on how much is spent.

Nokia's research and development activities are very strongly oriented toward product development. Even the corporate Research Center, which is responsible for the most basic research, is designed to be directly product-driven; this is ensured by the fact that it has to earn 70 percent of its finance by selling its research to the business research and development units, so that its activity is research for a customer. (The corporate level finances only 24 percent for long-term research; by comparison, the same figure at NEC is 70 percent. At Nokia, the

---

[17] The research and development figures are based on Buderi (2000); Nokia (2000c); and OECD (2001a). Some additional information has been obtained from interviews with Yrjö Neuvo, Executive Vice President, CTO of Mobile Phones, and Juhani Kuusi, Director of the Nokia Research Center.

remaining 6 percent comes from the public technology programs.) Nokia thinks that its focus should be on development-oriented research and that basic research belongs to the universities. Nokia's task is to network with them to share different types of knowledge. Thus Nokia closely networks with the top universities in Finland and elsewhere, both to learn from their basic research and to do more direct development-oriented projects with them (e.g., with MIT, Stanford University, the University of Tokyo, Beijing University of Post and Telecommunications, and Helsinki University of Technology).

It could be said that some of Nokia's research and development is outsourced to the universities, but this is again more a partnership than a traditional subcontracting. Nokia aims to retain a high level of internal expertise in different areas in order to critically evaluate research results. In all of this cooperation, it is considered essential to pick up signals about the future. This is a central motive in all networking, at a time when gaining indicators about the future from diverse sources is critical in order to move fast and see the big changes before others do. An additional benefit of these partnerships is that it gives Nokia the opportunity to attract the best talent from its partners, either by networking or by direct recruitment.

A central feature of the informational economy is that no single organization can have the research and development resources that the biggest efforts require. This is also true of Nokia. For very big research and development efforts Nokia has networked with other major companies, as in the cases of Bluetooth (wireless communication inside homes and offices with companies like Ericsson, Motorola, 3COM, Intel, IBM, Microsoft, and Toshiba); EPOC (operating system for mobile devices with Ericsson, Motorola, Psion, and Panasonic); Ipv6 (the development of a new Internet protocol to make it possible to connect everything from mobile phones to home appliances to the Net, a network comprising practically all major IT companies); and the public technology and standardization programs (such as the Finnish and the EU's technology programs, the Third Generation Partnership Programs for defining the next generation of mobile-phone standards, the World Wide Web Consortium that develops web standards; and so on).

At the beginning of 2001, Nokia had fifty-five research and development units in fifteen countries, linked very closely through the concept of virtual laboratories. The locations of the units are chosen so that research and development centers can be closer to the customers, and also in order to learn from the special expertise of each country (e.g., miniature technology in Japan, the recognition of Asian signs in China, the Internet in the United States, general mobile solutions in Finland, and so on). While less than 2 percent of Nokia's sales are in Finland, the contribution of the Finnish research and development nodes is still relatively high: 45 percent in the case of the most basic research of the corporate Research Center and 65 percent in the case of all research and development. Paradoxically, although Finland is generally a country of high labor costs, the salaries of highly educated Finnish research and development employees are much lower than, for example, in the United States.[18] However, it should also be noted that one-quarter of the employees of the Finnish Research Center are foreigners, so there is already a certain amount of internationalization of highly educated labor within Nokia in Finland.

Whereas, earlier Nokia acquired companies to expand its production capacity, after its transformation, Nokia's few and, relatively small acquisitions have been implemented mainly in order to acquire a critical mass of research and development capacity in some special new technology. The way of linking these acquired companies to the Nokia network varies: sometimes acquired companies continue their independent operation; and sometimes they are integrated more closely within the Nokia network.

*Management*

Many companies have moved toward the network enterprise model, but not all of them have been equally successful. The informational enterprise requires a new management style and this ability to manage networks seems to have been one of Nokia's strengths. In the 1990s, Nokia transformed itself into a flat organization with a decision hierarchy of just three levels in most cases: project, division, and the

[18] Väänänen (1996).

corporation. Nokia aims to be a meritocracy where people who have expertise in a particular area are included in decision-making, regardless of their formal status in the organization. Thus, decision networks are formed depending on each situation. Instead of management, Nokia often speaks of the "orchestration" of its core competence of research and development, production, and the brand.

Nokia also uses many methods to keep its network fully interactive and evolving. For example, the whole network is involved in the continuous "Nokia Way" strategy process (it is continuous in order to be more dynamic, just as Nokia's budget planning year has been reduced to six months to be more responsive to changing conditions). People at all levels think about what is important for the future and then, based on the flow of vision from the whole network, the top management gives it expression in the annual strategy presentation. The strategy is conceived in connection with the company's organization, which is purposefully kept in a constant state of change. This conscious and continuous thinking about the company's structure is considered an important innovation equal to its product innovations (Ollila says: "Structure drives strategy"). People are deliberately moved in the network, through job rotation, in order to share knowledge from one node to another and to avoid the forming of individual, closed knots. This applies both to people on the assembly line and to top management; for example, the presidents of Nokia Mobile Phones and Nokia Networks have been transferred from one division to another, although both divisions have been extremely profitable.

It could be added that Nokia's top five executives themselves form a decision-making network (in addition to Ollila, it includes President Pekka Ala-Pietilä, Nokia CFO Olli-Pekka Kallasvuo, Mobile Phones President Matti Alahuhta and Networks President Sari Baldauf, one of Finland's most visible female leaders). There is little hierarchy among them and, in fact, all key decisions are made together in a direct dialog. The interaction is kept both frequent and informal, and the "Top Five" drop into each other's offices on a daily basis to exchange thoughts. We might say that, instead of one person, Nokia is led by a "network CEO," although Ollila naturally remains the decision-maker of last resort.

*Nokia Values beyond Rhetorics*

Nokia considered it essential that its company culture was rethought during the same process as Nokia was transformed into a network enterprise: the "Nokia Values" provide the necessary new management culture for the network enterprise. The uniqueness of Nokia Values is that they were created by the Nokians themselves, by considering what had been the spirit behind Nokia's earlier strengths. Nokia Values were not a new wish list or something ordered from external consultants to improve the company image – the idea that "in these days every company has to have its values" – but they came from the company itself in the practical process of finding sources for the company's survival.

Four factors were articulated in the definition of Nokia Values: customer satisfaction, respect for the individual, achievement, and continuous learning. In practice, the values mean certain attitudes that are encouraged in recruitment, induction, and promotion. Customer satisfaction means the will to work together for the good of the customer. Respect for the individual means giving people responsibility and encouraging them to take risks in a culture of trust and frankness, where failing is also permitted. Achievement means the setting of creative "120 percent goals", in which some genuinely new thinking and an attitude of not surrendering to difficulties are required in order to achieve them. Continuous learning means that humility must be the norm, and being ready to constantly challenge and change one's thinking. Again, this thinking is given credibility by the attitude of the top management (e.g., some of their opening lines of discussion include "What is your most important recent insight?" and "Correct me if I'm wrong"). Naturally, there is always a gap between values in theory and practice, so the reality of the values depends constantly on the management's implementation of them. It is easy to understand that a very practical reason for seeing these values as important is the company's background in the conflictive and rarefied atmosphere that almost destroyed Nokia in the 1980s and early 1990s.

Nokia Values constitute the driving force for the network enterprise and feed its dynamism. They also provide a solid basis of identity to combine speedy external change and internal growth in the practice of Nokia's employees. The implementation of the values is assessed in annual development discussions ("360 degrees": managers give feedback to their workers, workers to their managers, and colleagues to each other), as well as with the help of employee surveys. They are also part of the continuous education in the company.

Nokia Values are not a fantasy world: they are strongly connected to financial discipline (in fact, the Nokia formulation of its principle is "value-based leadership and fact-based management"). The result of this multi-pronged transformation has been the growth of net sales by more than 35 percent a year and of the operating profit by more than 50 percent a year between 1996 and 2000. In 2000, when the economic downturn had already started, Nokia's net sales were 30.4 billion euros and its operating profit was 5.8 billion euros. Even in the more difficult year of 2001, Nokia has managed to make large operating profits, and to keep on winning market share from its competitors (at the end of summer 2001, Nokia's market share in mobile phones was over 35 percent).

## A Large Company in a Small Country? Nokia and Finland

Nokia's business model – focused product, linkage to global financial networks, and the network enterprise structure – is currently radiating to other companies in the Finnish IT cluster, beginning with Nokia's own suppliers and partners, which have turned themselves into global network enterprises with their own partner networks, and extending to the dozens of companies that are sprouting in the cluster.

As technological innovation and investment diffuse in the Finnish IT cluster, the cluster will probably also become increasingly diversified, and, correspondingly, Nokia's relative weight will decrease. Yet, as was underlined at the beginning of the chapter and reflected by the position given to Nokia in our analysis, for the time being Nokia holds a special position in the Finnish economy, which raises some concerns.

From the Finnish perspective, the first worry is: what would happen if Nokia left Finland for lower taxes? At present, less than

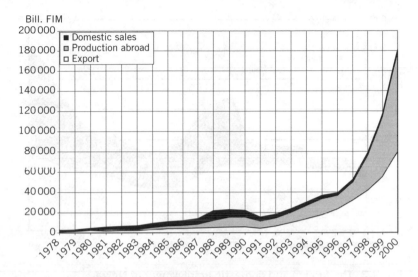

**Fig. 2.1** The net sales of Nokia (billion FIM)

*Source*: Etla.

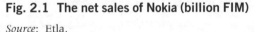

2 percent of Nokia's sales are in Finland, the majority of its labor force is in other countries, and 90 percent of Nokia is owned by foreign investors; so, on the surface, it would seem that Nokia is not tied to Finland (see Figs 2.1 and 2.2).

Still, it can be argued that it is not likely that Nokia will leave Finland. Nokia is a very Finnish company in terms of its culture and corporate identity. All the members of the top executive board are Finnish. Cultural homogeneity in the top echelons facilitates communication and trust. Feeling at home in Finland, in terms of government and institutional support, creates a safe platform from which to operate and experiment. Research and development are also rooted deeply in the Finnish innovation system. As established by empirical research, most leading companies in information technology are organized around certain milieux of innovation, Silicon Valley being the most famous of these.[19] Finland is the milieu of innovation where

---

[19] See Castells and Hall (1994).

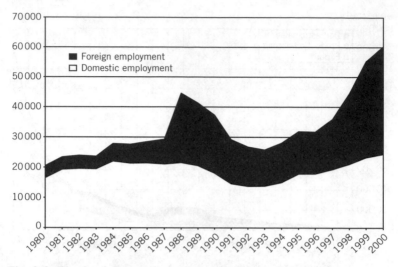

**Fig. 2.2  The foreign and domestic employment of Nokia**

*Source*: Etla.

Nokia thrives. So, to be Finnish for Nokia is not only a matter of identity: it also makes excellent business sense.

Another concern for Finland is: what would happen if Nokia failed?
Would that be catastrophic for the Finnish IT cluster or the Finnish
economy as a whole? At first glance, it might seem that the fate of
Finland is linked to the fate of Nokia – even to the extent that its citizens have also bet on Nokia for their individual future: the majority of
shares owned by Finns are Nokia shares and even those who do not
invest themselves cannot escape this link as Finnish pension funds
have put high stakes in Nokia.

However, here it is important to notice that Finland – not just
Nokia – has become a node in the global network of innovation, as
witnessed by the growing interest of other corporations to locate in
the area or to find connections with Finnish companies (which also
means that even if Nokia moved its headquarters away from Finland
it would still continue to have a strong presence in Finland). So, in the
unlikely event of a catastrophic failure by Nokia, similar to the one
that nearly happened at the beginning of the 1990s, parts of Nokia
would be taken up by new, or existing, companies – just as Nokia itself

has collected parts of Finnish IT expertise throughout its history. Finnish expertise could also be networked through channels other than Nokia.

Nor is the Finnish economy as a whole dependent on Nokia, although failure by Nokia would require difficult adaptation. At the beginning of 2001, Nokia employed about 25 000 workers in Finland, which was about 1 percent of total employment – still a limited impact on the labor market. Nokia's suppliers and partners would add about 20 000 jobs but, just like Nokia's own employees, these suppliers could (and do) work as well for other companies – and there is constantly more demand than supply for IT professionals in Finland. Thus, all in all, Nokia's employment contribution is not decisive.

This is also true of the indicators that are often referred to in the context of arguing that Nokia has too much influence in Finland. In the year 2000, Nokia accounted for some 70 percent of Finland's IT exports and nearly 25 percent of total exports. But here analysts often overlook the fact that most international trade these days (about two-thirds worldwide) takes place within multinational corporations and their ancillary networks and this is likely to be the case for Nokia. In fact, international trade is more an indicator of the internationalization of production, rather than the lifeline of a bounded national economy. As long as Finland is integrated in the global production network of IT goods and services, there will be exports (and imports as well) in information technology, with or without Nokia. Similarly misleading is the fact that Nokia accounts for about two-thirds of the value of stocks traded on the Helsinki Stock Exchange. This tells us more about how small the Helsinki Stock Exchange is than about the size of Nokia. Since in all likelihood the Helsinki Stock Exchange (together with all other European exchanges) will be merged in one of the two or three mega-exchanges currently being formed, this benchmark will simply vanish.

Also, the idea that Finland creates its policies for Nokia is not supported by empirical evidence. True, the importance of Nokia in the Finnish economy and for the image of Finland in the world is an obvious factor that any decision-maker weighs in his or her judgment on specific policies. Policy-makers in telecommunications, taxation, immigration, education, Internet literacy, trade, and many other key areas, take the interests of the IT cluster, with Nokia at its core, into consideration. But most of the issues that are important to Nokia – such as the lowering of taxes for temporary foreign personnel to bring Nokia into line with global conditions – actually represent the wider interests of the IT sector, which Finland has to take into consideration in order to create general conditions for success in the informational economy.

In fact, Finland could not cater for the special political interests of Nokia even if it wanted to because the Finnish state has, by and large, given up much of its sovereignty to the political networks of the EU – as is the case with all other European member states. This is not to say that there is no national government anymore but that national governments have to operate within a network of institutions, laws, agreements, treaties, alliances, strategies, and compromises: the European network state. In the transnational decision-making process of the European network state, Nokia cannot have more special political treatment than its competitors like Ericsson, Siemens, Alcatel, Phillips, and the like. In fact, the world in which the United States shaped its policies based on the interests of General Motors ("What's good for General Motors is good for America") has vanished, not only for Finland, Nokia, and Europe, but for the United States itself. Ultimately, all of them depend on global networks.

So, to sum up: Nokia is central to Finland but not in the sense that Finland is entirely economically dependent upon or politically subordinated to Nokia. Nokia's important role in Finland is to act as the current channel for Finnish IT expertise. Nokia is a product of Finland and Finland's economy is partly driven by Nokia's innovation and competitiveness, but they are both dependent on a world of global networks in which their ties, for the time being, represent a major asset both for the company and the country.

# Chapter 3

# INNOVATION ABOUT INNOVATING

## The Unlikely Innovation System: The State, Corporate Business, Universities, and Hackers

*Innovation as the Ultimate Driver of Informationalism*

The informational economy is driven by informational financial markets, enterprises, and the labor force. Market value is the core but in the long run a company's market value can only be based on profits and, at the bottom, economic growth is built on productivity growth.

## Innovation about Innovating

And the ultimate source of productivity growth is innovation: product, process, and organizational innovation.

Behind these innovations are – regardless of whether we talk about innovation in the private, public, or citizen sector – educated people, a functioning financing system, and a culture of innovation. Educated innovators range from university researchers to R&D workers within companies to creative individual citizens. The public sector has to invest to a high level in science and education in order to have innovators in the universities and outside of them. Business innovation requires additional advanced systems of funding. And, although citizen innovation is predominantly not driven by money, to be able to put their energy to innovating, individuals have to ensure at least a minimum financial level in their life.

But education and money alone are not sufficient; a culture of innovation is also needed. We call it the "hacker ethic" following Himanen's *The Hacker Ethic and the Spirit of the Information Age*.[1] Here, the word "hacker" does not have any connection with computer criminals but means – as it originally did – an individual who wishes to realize his or her creative passion: a hacker is driven by an idea whose realization he or she feels is important in itself, even energizing and enjoyable. Hackers want to realize themselves fully, to use their special creative capabilities, to constantly surpass themselves, and to produce creative work as a result of their actions. On a social level, hackers work as a network, in which development work is kept open to a degree in which others can join in the realization of the idea.

The hacker ethic as a culture of innovation becomes increasingly significant in the informational age, in which the ultimate source of growth is creativity or innovation. The work culture of the industrial age, the so-called Protestant ethic, which taught that work should be seen as a duty in which one does a given part and in which suffering is even noble, well suited the needs of the industrial economy, in which many jobs were routine and the resulting work a direct function of the used energy (time). But this old work culture operates very badly in the informational economy, in which the work's result is a function of creativity.

---

[1] Himanen (2001).

For companies, the fact that their product is a function of their employees' creativity means that their challenge is to develop a company culture that beats other companies in the competition to recruit, keep, and use best the creative experts. The hacker ethic is also the innovation culture that drives the researchers on whose theories business innovations are ultimately built. And the same attitude powers the citizen innovators in the so-called open-source movement (the hackers in the word's most original sense).

In global competition, the idea of networking included in the hacker ethic is crucial because the most fundamental innovations require such huge resources that no single actor can have them alone – regardless of whether we talk about enterprises, researchers, or citizens. In global competition, one is not a revolution but a network of rebels is needed. And others will not join in the network of rebels unless there is some degree of openness in the development. For business this means that if a company does not open its innovation sufficiently and fast enough for others to join in innovating, even a great innovation does not stand much chance of success but remains an outdated secret in the hands of the company. This is because in the closed model the pace of innovation is reduced to the pace of one company's resources. Of course, this may not be a problem for the company for years. But the history of technology has plenty of examples of how, in the long run, the closed model has lost to the open model. One can recall how Apple's technologically much more advanced closed architecture lost to IBM PC's inferior open architecture, or how Sony's more developed but closed Betamax video standard lost to the less developed but open VHS standard. Later in this chapter, we will analyze how the open NMT/GSM mobile network standards conferred an advantage on the European (and Finnish) telecommunications companies compared to the American companies that believed more in the closed model, and how the open Internet/Web standards beat their closed competitors.

Naturally, we are talking here about openness that can have varying degrees. In business, openness is often limited to standards and companies otherwise close off their innovations. Some companies believe that "basic technology;" that is, the lowest level of implementation of the standards, such as the network technology (e.g., Internet protocols), or operating systems (e.g., Linux), is also best left to develop openly. This is not only because of the vast resources that are needed but also because a popular close implementation of open standards is the way in which open standards can be captured and gradually transformed into closed standards (e.g., introducing non-standard features to a popular Web browser would be the most efficient way of slowly closing off the Web standard). At its extreme, openness is a principle that permeates everything, including the applications, as in the case of researchers and the most ideological citizen hackers. Of course, few companies adopt such a radical approach.

At the national level, the growing significance of networking for innovation means that, for a country, the critical question is what kind of innovation network its public, private, and citizen sectors form together. The nature of this national innovation system creates the preconditions for its economy's success, which also means that innovations about the innovation system can confer an important national competitive advantage.

## The Genesis of the Finnish Innovation System

Behind the most immediate sources of Finland's technological and economic growth – a focus on information technology, the linking of national companies and the economy to global financial markets, and the network enterprise structure – is the specific national innovation system, which has produced success stories like Nokia and Linux.[2] Let us approach the Finnish innovation system by first describing the genesis of the main public elements of this system.[3] The 1960s were

[2] For a discussion of the concept of the national innovation system, see Freeman (1987); Porter (1990); Lundvall (1992); Nelson (1993); Edquist (1997); Archibugi and Lundvall (2001). An important point to emphasize here is that when we focus on the national level of the innovation system we do not want to deny that in the informational economy innovation processes also have important global and local levels.

[3] There has been considerable research on the Finnish innovation system following the introduction of the concept in Finland in 1990 by the Science and Technology Policy Council. Three main loci of research include the VTT group for technology research (e.g., Lemola, 2001), Etla (e.g., Vuori and Vuorinen, 1994), and Sitra (Miettinen *et al.*, 1999; Schienstock and Kuusi, 1999; Schienstock and Hämäläinen, 2001).

the time when the basis of the Finnish university system was strengthened and its finance improved: in fact, until then, Finland had full universities in only two cities. The national Science Policy Council was founded in 1963, and the organization and financing of the Finnish Academy was renewed in 1969 under the Ministry of Education. As a result, in the 1970s, there were twenty public, free, high-quality universities in ten cities, guided by the Science Policy Council and funded by the Finnish Academy.

The Finnish National Fund for Research and Development, Sitra, was founded in 1967 with considerable freedom to pursue its own way of advancing the economy through direct financing of companies and its own creative projects. One of Sitra's projects, Pertti Kohi's *Technology Assessment* in 1976, was very influential in the discussion of technology policy in the atmosphere of recession. Its publication also coincided with the first years of the IT revolution, which had just begun to attract international attention. In this general atmosphere, a number of visionary committees were founded, including the Technology Committee in 1979.[4] As a result of their analyses, the need for a conscious national technology policy was increasingly identified and action was soon taken.

In 1982, the government made the decision-in-principle to raise national research and development investment from 1.2 percent of GDP to 2.2 percent by 1992.[5] The National Technology Agency, Tekes, was founded in 1983 to finance technology research and development as an independent agency that reports to the Ministry of Trade and Industry.[6] And in 1986 the government's Science Policy Council was transformed into the more holistic and practical Science and Technology Policy Council.[7] Finland met its 1982 technology policy research and development investment goal in 1992 and set new, higher goals. In 1996, still partly suffering from the recent recession,

---

[4] Also cf. Nevalainen (1999).
[5] Decision-in-principle of the Council of State 727/140/82 VNK.
[6] Tekes was founded on the basis of the work of the so-called Raate Committee.
[7] This was based on the government's reports to Parliament on Finland's science and technology policy in 1985: "The activities of the Science Policy Council of Finland are to be revised so as to enhance its capacity for acting as a coordinating body between the various ministries in the field of technology policy as well."

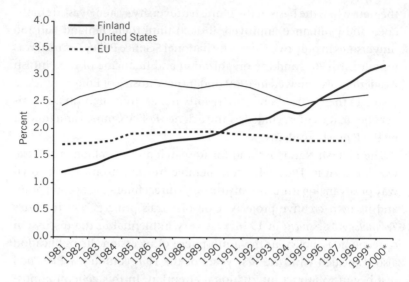

**Fig. 3.1  Research and development investment in Finland, the United States, and the EU, 1981–2000 (percent of GDP)**

*Note*:  The * indicates an estimate.

the Finnish government nevertheless decided to further increase research and development investment to 2.9 percent of GDP by 1999, although it was otherwise cutting public expenditure.[8] This goal was reached in 1998 and currently the share is estimated to be 3.2 percent, making Finland, with Sweden, world leaders in research and development investment as measured by the share of GDP (Fig. 3.1).[9]

## The Science and Technology Policy Council: The Strategic Actor

All of these elements have continued to be key factors in the Finnish innovation system. The main source of this conscious and continuous research and development policy is the government's Science and

---

[8]  Science and Technology Policy Council (1996*b*).
[9]  Prihti *et al.* (2000); see also Asplund (2000).

Technology Policy Council.[10] It has been influential in advancing both the human and the financial bases for innovation by emphasizing the need for high-quality university education and research in the field of technology, the need to increase national R&D investment, and the need to encourage an open innovation culture through the regulatory environment.

The working model of the Finnish Science and Technology Policy Council is very exceptional when viewed from an international perspective. Many countries have science policy councils but the Finnish council is organized directly under the Prime Minister who also chairs the council's meetings. It is not a stereotypical committee, which just discusses things and writes papers, but is a serious body that includes eight key ministers (the Ministers of Education and of Trade and Industry are the vice-chairmen) and ten of the highest-level representatives of Finnish universities (rectors and top researchers), industry (e.g., at present, Nokia's CEO), the Academy, Tekes, and employers' and employees' organizations (at director level). The shared vision spreads to the key participating bodies from the top down. The other central difference from other countries is that in Finland science and technology are treated together – in the same council.

## Technology-oriented Universities: The Source of Talented People

The human basis of the Finnish innovation system is university education and research. Partly through the influence of the Science and Technology Policy Council (financed through Tekes and the Academy), Finnish education is very technology-centered. Out of all students, 27 percent are in science, mathematics, and engineering, which is twice the number of that in most comparable countries.[11]

---

[10] For a brief introduction to the council, see *http://www.minedu.fi/ minedu/research/ organisation/sci_tech_council/sci_tech_council.html*. For substance, see its reviews: the Science and Technology Policy Council (1987, 1990, 1993, 1996*a,b*, 2000). We have also gained further information from our discussions with the former and current secretaries of the Council, Erkki Ormala, and Kimmo Halme.

[11] Cf. UNDP (2001).

In 1998, an additional program to increase the information-industry education was launched by the Ministry of Education in accordance with the council's proposal.

The Helsinki University of Technology (HUT) is clearly the most important public research institution in the technology field, but Tampere University of Technology and the University of Oulu have also become similar drivers and spatial centers of technology research and development. In addition to the universities, the public research institution Technical Research Center (VTT) is important.

## Tekes: The Research and Development Fund

The Academy is focused on funding basic research but it has close links with Tekes, which has become the main channel for business-oriented public research and development finance.[12] According to international evaluations, Tekes has been very efficient in funding research and development that aims at exportable products; in practice, it has funded all successful Finnish technology companies at some point in their development (including Nokia). From an international perspective, Tekes' strength is its strong independent status. In many other countries similar activities are organized by the parliament or the relevant ministry, but Tekes has significant autonomy. Although Tekes is responsible to the Ministry of Trade and Industry, the ministry cannot take decisions on funding; Tekes makes the decisions itself. This independence has allowed Tekes to act both swiftly and with a much longer perspective than if it were part of the political structure. In this way, decision-making is also much closer to the actual research and development world.

Tekes acts both proactively and reactively. Through its technology programs, Tekes raises new themes where it identifies a need for research and development. These programs are designed together with the universities and companies, and they include steering groups with representatives from research, industry, and the government.

[12] For an evaluation of Tekes, see Prihti et al. (2000). For general information, see www.tekes.fi. We have received additional information from the current and former Director Generals of Tekes: Veli-Pekka Saarnivaara and Juhani Kuusi.

Tekes is also open to project proposals, which do not fit into its technology programs, and funds them if they meet its criteria of being technologically and economically promising *and* include cooperation between other companies or universities. So new initiatives originate both from the top down and from the bottom up.

Networking is strongly rewarded both in the special technology programs and in individual projects: the more networking there is between large companies, between large companies and small or middle-sized companies, between small and middle-sized companies, and between companies and universities, the higher the Tekes share of funding will be (it can rise from a basic 50 to 70 percent). As a result of this networking model, Tekes has accumulated considerable knowledge capital about what research and development are being carried out in universities and companies and which issues are regarded as the main future challenges. Through the direction of its resources, Tekes indirectly shares this knowledge capital (sometimes it even suggests cooperation to companies that it thinks would profit from interaction).

Tekes tries to retain its dynamism by constantly evaluating itself and the projects it funds. For example, each technology program is evaluated at its completion by its steering group. Tekes also tries to remain small (presently it has about two hundred members of staff) and flat in organization.

## Sitra: The Public Capitalist

The founding of Tekes for the very specific goal of advancing technology research and development work has also had the positive impact of clarifying the role of Sitra.[13] Since Tekes was founded, Sitra has not funded technology research and development *per se*, but has evolved into a venture capitalist that finances the beginning and

[13] For general information, see *www.sitra.fi*. We have received additional information from: Aatto Prihti President of Sitra; Research Director Antti Hautamäki; Development Manager Timo Hämäläinen, and Training Director Tapio Anttila.

expansion phases of start-up companies. Thus, Tekes and Sitra form a combination that helps innovation in the crucial early stages. In fact, 95 percent of the companies that Sitra has invested in have first been partners of Tekes and, in order to achieve the best possible results, there is close cooperation between Tekes and Sitra at all levels. Since the private venture capital market became well developed in the late 1990s in Finland, Sitra has started to emphasize pre-seed financing.

In addition to its role as the biggest venture capitalist in Finland, Sitra is a think-tank that innovates new ideas (it had an important role in the idea of the creation of Tekes) and finances thought-provoking research that is not product oriented and education in areas that it sees as important for Finland (it may also finance experiments in these areas). Sitra's strategic work includes, among other things, strategic education about new challenges for small groups of top-level people from different types of organization (currently the so-called "Finland 2015" groups, which are distinctive in that they are able to bring together the top people from government, business, and research for discussions and fact-finding trips to centers like Washington, DC, Silicon Valley, Brussels, and Moscow), and the renewal of the Finnish information-society strategy in 1998 through a process that involved hundreds of experts from research, industry, and the public sector. Sitra's specialty is to be a "public capitalist" and a "public think-tank."

As Sitra is responsible to the Finnish Parliament, it can be thought of as an agent of a shared national project. However, this relation to Parliament does not mean direct control: in fact, like Tekes, Sitra has autonomous status. And, also like Tekes, Sitra is more a network organization than a big institution. At the time of writing, it has only about sixty employees.

## Innovation Culture: Open Regulatory Environment and Standards

In addition to educated people (taken care of by the universities) and finance (taken care of by Tekes and Sitra), the third key element in innovation is the innovation culture. For the state, it means advancing a regulatory environment that is open to innovation. The Finnish state has taken an active role in liberalization, deregulation, and privatization – without taking this to an extreme. Key events for the technology industry include the separation of the national Post, Telephone, and Telegraph company from its regulatory function in 1987; the opening up of mobile communications service provision in 1990, making Finland the first country in the world to have a commercial GSM operator; and integration with EU regulation in 1997.[14] This open regulatory environment created a forerunner position for Finnish companies.

The government has also furthered open standards in a way that has given a competitive advantage to Finnish telecommunications companies. The Finnish Post, Telegraph, and Telephone company played a key role with other Nordic public telecom companies in the development of a new transnational mobile phone standard, and thus in creating the biggest mobile phone network and market of its time in the world (60–70 percent of the worldwide subscription in 1982–3).[15] The decision to form a group to develop a new mobile phone standard was made during the conference of the Nordic public telecompanies in 1969. There was a joint agreement for a common standard among Nordic countries, although the formal initiator was Sweden (which at the time had the most knowledge of telecommunications in Scandinavia thanks to Ericsson). The group was called "Nordiska Mobiltelefongruppen" (Nordic Mobile Telephone group, NMT), and it later gave its name to the network as well. Initially, the informal NMT group consisted of just one to four representatives from each Nordic country (except Iceland). Later on, when the NMT group had been divided into several subgroups to address specific problems, these groups functioned by getting together for an intensive week of work. All standards or specifications have been openly available. The NMT group wanted to involve others in the development process from the start, and thus it was very open to ideas from the equipment manufacturers.

[14] For a more detailed description of this development, see Turpeinen (1996b) and Steinbock (2000).
[15] According to Pulkkinen (1996). For the history of the Nordic Mobile Telephone (NMT) standard, see Miettinen *et al.* (1999). Also cf. Toivola (1992).

The Finnish government took a very active role in pushing the Finnish telecommunications industry behind the open standard. When the decision to build the NMT network had been made, Nokia (or, more precisely, Mobira, which was founded by merging Nokia's and Salora's radio-technology divisions, and which later became part of Nokia) put forward a proposal that was technically insufficient. Instead of just rejecting it, the Finnish Post and Telecommunications Administration helped Nokia to develop its proposal, introducing Nokia to Radio System Sweden AB, which was able to subcontract for the manufacturing of the necessary base station combiners. It can be said that the Finnish government played a significant part in making Nokia what it is today, in the same sense that Nordic NMT cooperation created the basis of future success for all Nordic telecom companies: the Nordic mobile phone network gave Nordic companies a unique opportunity to develop an advantage in mobile communications expertise, which they were able to retain when they promoted the common European (and later wider) completely digital GSM standard (the Finnish Radiolinja was the first to launch the service in 1991) and its successors like UMTS (Finland was the first to grant licenses in 1999, without auctions). Also, the fact that the NMT standard was open benefited the Finnish and Nordic telecom companies because it made development highly competitive: Nokia and Ericsson had to compete with each other and other big companies like Motorola, Mitsubishi, Panasonic, NEC, and Siemens.

## The Historical Conditions of Innovation in Telecommunications

Of course, it would be wrong to give the impression that everything in Finland's development into a leading telecommunications country has been deliberate public strategy or has been motivated by the economy. Some factors relate clearly to the country's history and have a political dimension. This is the case in the story of how the Finnish telecommunications industry became the world's most openly competitive one.[16] Finland was an autonomous province of Russia until

---

[16] For the early history of telecommunications in Finland, see Moisala *et al.* (1977); Turpeinen (1996*a,b*).

1917. Russia controlled international telegraph lines, which it considered to be militarily critical. The Finns wanted to take control of telecommunications, which they related to independence, but in the 1850s Russia rejected the proposal to give this control to the Finnish Telegraph Office. To avoid the story of Russian control repeating itself in local telephone communication, the Finnish Senate decided in 1879 to leave telephone operation in the private sector. In most other countries, the telephone was considered to be a successor to the telegraph and thereby a state monopoly. In 1886, the Finnish Senate issued a telephone statute, which distinguished sharply between telephone and telegraph regulation. The statute was motivated by the political considerations of advancing Finnish interests as much as possible within Russia.

As a result, Finland was very enthusiastic about the telephone and got its first telephone line in 1877, a year after Bell's invention. By 1881, Bell, Ericsson, and Siemens and Halske were operating in Finland, in addition to Finnish companies such as Daniel Johannes Wadén's Helsinki Telephone Corporation, now known as Elisa Communications. Through the presence of international companies Finland also gained global expertise in an area in which foreign companies remained leaders until the end of the 1980s. Just before World War II there were 815 telephone companies in Finland. This historical background means that Finnish telecommunication companies experienced a competitive market and demanding customers, which forced them to be technologically advanced and very customer-focused, in contrast to many other countries where there was a protected relationship between the monopolistic public tele-operator and manufacturer. These historical circumstances also created a strong consciousness of telecommunications as a strategic matter, which has proved beneficial long after the original political reasons have faded away. The early competition was for historically determined *political* reasons, but in the 1980s competition also became a conscious *economic* goal.

There was also an important political dimension to the Finnish interest in the IT revolution, which began in the US. The reason Finland was so interested in joining the European technology programs of the 1980s was not only to do with technological goals but also formed a neutral way of becoming more and more associated with the West (in a way that would not provoke protest from the Soviet Union). Ironically, the problems associated with this slow integration did not arise from the East but from the West. For example, when the European technology program EUREKA was started in 1985, all EFTA (European Free Trade Association) countries were invited to the inaugural meeting in addition to the EU countries, except for Finland whose YYA Treaty (Treaty of Friendship, Cooperation, and Mutual Assistance) with the Soviet Union was understood to mean that all technological information given to Finland would flow directly to the Soviet Union. Finland managed to attend the meeting but only after considerable political maneuvering. Similar problems were encountered in joining other European technology cooperation programs before the collapse of the Soviet Union.

## Business Innovation

The public sector ultimately creates conditions for the other key players in the innovation system: the corporations. Tekes has had an increasing impact on business research and development as companies have to match its investment. The growth of business research and development has also been encouraged by the positive research and development environment created by bodies like the Science and Technology Policy Council. But, of course, business also increases its research and development investments independently and for direct business reasons. Ultimately, the research and development investment of the most successful companies, such as Nokia in Finland's case, become positive examples for other businesses. As a result, in 1999, the private sector accounted for 69 percent of all Finnish research and development, up from 57 percent in 1991 (Fig. 3.2).[17]

The development of Nokia provides a good example of the interaction between private and public (government and university) elements of the innovation system. In the 1960s, Nokia – or, to be precise, the Finnish Cable Works – had already founded a radio-technology

---

[17] Prihti *et al.* (2000); see also Asplund (2000).

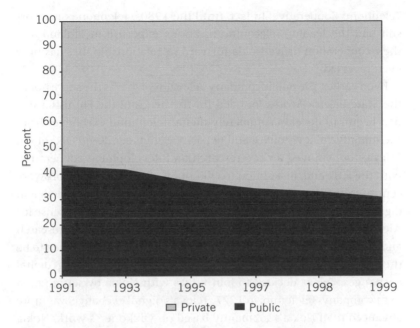

Fig. 3.2 Public and private research and development investment, 1991–9

Source: Prihti et al. (2000).

laboratory for researching the future, which might be wireless, on the initiative of its CEO. Soon after, the company evolved into one of Finland's biggest concentrations of IT expertise.[18] The radio-technology laboratory was a place of pioneering spirit that attracted university professors and young engineers. From the beginning, it had particularly close relations with the HUT.

After the merger in 1966, Nokia was one of the biggest companies in Finland with more resources to direct into research and development investments. Thus, although the radio-technology department was not financially profitable, it was allowed to continue its development work. The laboratory's first focus was on telephone centers – work in which Nokia benefited greatly from its cooperation with such demanding but patient customers as the national Post, Telephone, and Telegraph company, Helsinki Telephone Cooperative, and Tampere

[18] Cf. Lovio (1996).

Telephone Cooperative. In fact, until the 1980s, telephone operators still had the leading telecommunications expertise in Finland and their cooperation drove Nokia forward (a relationship that has now been reversed).

Even earlier, the public company Televa, which was the successor to the State Electric Works founded for the needs of the Finnish army, had begun to develop completely digital telephone exchanges from the initiative of a visionary and persistent engineer, Keijo Olkkonen. Televa, too, enjoyed a close research and development cooperation with the HUT and, in addition to Olkkonen, two of its professors were central to the development work. Nokia had acquired knowledge in digital telecommunications by purchasing a manufacturing license for Alcatel's digital exchange in 1977, and it also began its own research and development project on digital exchanges. As Nokia seemed to be the most promising private company for commercializing digital exchanges, Televa decided to join forces with Nokia by setting up a joint company, Telefenno, in 1977. Televa's digital exchange was more advanced than Nokia's so, mainly based on Olkkonen's work, Nokia achieved its first success in digital telecommunications, the DX200 digital exchange. Finally, Nokia was allowed to acquire Telefenno completely. In this way, the government transferred public expertise to the private sector.

Parallel to Nokia's work in its other central innovative field, portable radio phones, another Finnish company called Salora was also undertaking development work. Salora's mobile phone, which was developed by the passionate engineer, Jorma Nieminen, was again more advanced than Nokia's product.[19] The public sector also played a part in Nokia's development from this starting-point to eventually becoming the leader in mobile phones. Of course, the final step was based on Nokia's ability as one of Finland's biggest companies, to acquire the knowledge from Salora, but this happened in a setting staged by actors in the public sector. In 1963, the Finnish Army issued a call for tenders for technologically sophisticated radio phones, which prompted both Nokia (then Finnish Cable Works) and Salora to develop

---

[19] For the history of Finnish radio phone manufacturing, see also Koivusalo (1995).

their research into these products. Then in 1979, when the national Post, Telephone, and Telegraph company invited the Finnish radio-technology companies to a dinner to discuss the forthcoming NMT network, Nokia and Salora agreed on cooperation, which led to the founding of their joint company, Mobira. Before long, Nokia was wealthy enough to take over this company entirely.

So Nokia's first steps to becoming a world leader in telecommunications was based as much on its cooperation with the public sector and on acquiring expertise from other private companies as on its own internal research and development work, not to mention the close relations with university researchers, which also made it possible for Nokia to recruit the most talented young engineering students. When Nokia acquired Mobira in 1982, it had collected the key Finnish expertise in telecommunications equipment manufacturing within it. This is the reason why Nokia can be seen as the expression of a collective Finnish expertise in the telecommunications technology. The public sector had deliberately pushed Nokia into becoming the channel for the network of this expertise. In this sense, Nokia is a truly national project. Nokia is an example of how private companies have turned Finnish know-how, created by the universities and communicated by public companies, into products by providing the necessary financial basis.

Since the appointment of Ollila as CEO in 1992, Nokia has been driven primarily by its own internal research and development, making only one major acquisition by buying the British mobile phone manufacturer Technophone (from which it learned mostly about production) in addition to acquiring some relatively small Internet companies mainly in the US. In the 1990s and the beginning of this century, the most important public contributions from Nokia's viewpoint have been cooperation with the universities and the liberal regulatory environment.

## The Users as Innovators

Although interaction between the public and private sectors has been the main source of technological innovation, we should not forget the role of the civil society in innovation. In fact, corporations and states have often been surprised by the actual uses that people develop for new technology. The history of the telephone, following its invention by Bell in 1876, provides a good example. At first, the telephone was marketed as a survival tool for emergencies. An advertisement from the 1920s dramatized the fears of a "home alone" housewife: "my heart stood still . . . I heard stealthy voices . . . someone tinkering with a lock . . . a muffled footstep . . . saw a shadow flit by my window . . . I reached over to the stand by the bedside and seized – no, not a revolver – a telephone." The telephone companies' view of the telephone as a means to send emergency messages was even reflected in the billing: calls were referred to as "messages." Early advocates of the telephone also proposed a high-level cultural use for the new technology: people would be able to listen to concerts. Bell and his assistant Watson would often demonstrate their invention by transmitting music over the lines.

Claude S. Fischer's *America Calling: A Social History of the Telephone to 1940* demonstrates how an understanding of the social dimension only dawned upon the marketers in the late 1920s.[20] Even then, the first advertisements showing social telephone calls always involved the transmission of some message – an invitation or congratulations – rather than people just wanting to talk to each other without any pre-determined subject or clear outcome. People, however, from the very beginning adopted the telephone as a tool for social interaction.

In the history of the mobile phone, similar surprises have been encountered. Its initial marketing strategy was very similar to that of its stationary predecessor, emphasizing, for example, how a mobile phone is a handy tool in emergency situations on the road and so on. Although Nokia included text messaging in its mobile phones and was in this sense the inventor of it, Nokia was greatly surprised by the lively messaging culture that the Finnish people created. The inventors of text messaging did not really expect anyone to start using the max-160-characters messaging except for the transmission of very urgent messages (for which reason the service is called SMS, "short messaging service").

[20]  Fischer (1992).

However, at the time of writing, five million Finns send more than a billion text messages per year.[21] This new communication culture, which spread to other countries when they achieved similar levels of mobile phone penetration, was created in particular by young users.[22] Text messages are used, among other things, for coordinating activities (e.g., telling friends that you are in a particular restaurant if others happen to be close by) or even for expressing love (a study of text messaging includes this love letter in 160 characters: "WILL U START DATING WITH ME? I REALLY LUV YOU . . . IF I'VE ASKED THIS EARLIER I DON'T REMEMBER YOUR ANSWER. PS. [I'M NOT DRUNK].)"[23]

## Hackers as Innovators

Citizen innovation, which Finnish telecommunication companies nowadays consciously want to link-up with, is very close to the innovations of hackers in the history of the Internet (including in this concept its predecessor Arpanet), another example of innovation independent of corporations and states. As is well known, the US government, through the Ministry of Defence Advanced Research Projects Agency (ARPA), was behind the building of the Net, but the governmental vision of the Net was related to survival and to science. In the late 1960s, Paul Baran, a researcher with RAND, the research center of the US air force, had a vision of a Net able to survive nuclear attack, and later described it as follows: "If the strategic weapons command and control systems could be more survivable, then the country's retaliatory capability could better allow it to withstand an attack and still function; a more stable position." Baran's goal was a

---

[21] Ministry of Transportation and Communications (2001).

[22] There is not much international research on the subject. One of the few is Townsend (2000). However, numerous Finnish studies have been published on the subject, including most importantly Kasesniemi and Rautiainen (2001), which is based on very extensive empirical data about young people's mobile communication culture. The empirical literature also includes Coogan and Kangas (2001) and Ketamo et al. (2000a and b). For more theoretical perspectives, there are Kopomaa (2000 a and b) and Mäenpää (2000).

[23] Quoted in Kasesniemi and Rautiainen (2001).

network in which the transmission of orders could be secured in emergencies. This premise was reflected in the name he gave to his concept: "Distributed Adaptive Message Block Network" (once again, there is the notion of "message").

Baran's reports did not, however, lead directly to the Arpanet and to its successor, the Internet. The Arpanet was not constructed according to RAND's vision but followed another military agency, ARPA's own. Jane Abbate, in *Inventing the Internet*, states that ARPA's director Lawrence Roberts was not "concerned with survivability." Roberts envisaged a Net in which "in particular fields or disciplines it will be possible to achieve a 'critical mass' of talent by allowing geographically separated people to work effectively in interaction with a system."[24] Writing about the history of the Internet, Roberts has gone so far as to call the notion that the motivation for the Arpanet was the creation of a nuclear-attack proof net a "false rumor."[25] The loftier governmental vision for the Arpanet, which he represents, intended it to be a tool for computer science.

Hackers, with a college student background, transformed the Net into a social innovation. As early as 1970, Carr, Crocker, and Cerf, student hackers in the Network Working Group, which started to develop the Arpanet through an open development process, noted that the Net was creating a new kind of social experience: "We have found that, in the process of connecting machines and operating systems together, a great deal of rapport has been established between personnel at various network node sites. The resulting mixture of ideas, discussions, disagreements, and resolutions has been highly refreshing and beneficial to all involved, and we regard the human interaction as a valuable by-product of the main effort."

This experience soon led to practical applications, and the social "by-product" became the first Net hit. Very soon after, hacker Ray Tomlinson devised the first electronic mail in 1972, which became the most favored use of the Net. Since then, e-mail accounts for more than three-quarters of the total use of the Net. In 1979, students Tom Truscott, Jim Ellis, and Steve Bellovin at Duke and the University of North Carolina developed newsgroups. And, beginning in 1990, Tim

---

[24] Abbate (1999).    [25] Leiner *et al.* (2000).

Berners-Lee and other hackers joined forces in an open development process that created the World Wide Web, which is how the Net is now known to most users. It should be added that, as Jane Abbate has shown, it was the openness of the Net standards that made it a winner in the competition for the network of networks.

The role of hacker innovation in the history of the Internet is import-ant because, in Finland, hackers have had an especially big part to play. In fact, they should be given special attention in any attempt to understand what is unique about the Finnish milieu of innovation. There are three important factors related to the history of the Internet. First, it was hackers who brought the Internet to Finland in the begin-ning and advanced its spread more rapidly than anywhere else. Second, Finnish hackers have made an important contribution to the Net's transformation into a social medium. And, third, Finnish hack-ers have played a crucial role in the development of a new innovation system: the open-source development model.

*Hackers as Internet Pioneers*

Although many hackers were important in linking Finland to the Internet, three deserve special mention here: Juha Heinänen, a young computer scientist at Tampere University of Technology; Harri Salminen, a student at the HUT; and Johan (Julf) Helsingius, an active Finnish Unix User Group member.[26] The first national university net-work was funded by Sitra in 1971 and it has been continuously upgraded to be at the cutting edge technologically. By 1984, the net-work had evolved into Funet or the Finnish University and Research Network. However, it was left to the Finnish hackers to take the ini-tiative in linking the Finnish network to international networks. The first step was taken by the pioneers of the Finnish Unix User Group who set up a link to the European Unix User Group network, Eunet (by UUCP or Unix to Unix Copy). The first official Finnish Eunet node was hosted by Helsingius' company Penetron in 1985. The first actual Internet link was the result of the efforts of Juha Heinänen, who had

---

[26] For the history of the Finnish Internet, see Häikiö (1995) and Käpyaho (1996). We have also gained additional information from the histories that have been published on the Net (Järvinen, 1994; Salminen, 1999) as well as from discussions with the key actors, Juha Heinänen, Harri Salminen, and Johan Helsingius.

**Innovation about Innovating**

already played a part in the establishment of the Finnish Eunet node, and Harri Salminen, who had become the technical coordinator of Funet and backed Heinänen.

Heinänen contacted the US Internet developers and suggested that an Internet link could be established from Finland to the US through the Nordic network, Nordunet. Eventually this happened and in 1988 Nordic countries became the first to have national networks connected to the Internet, but not without political difficulties. Finland's route to the Internet faced a similar obstacle to that encountered in joining the European technology programs: the first American reaction to Heinänen's suggestion was negative because Finland was seen as an ally of the Soviet Union. Larry Landweber of the NSFNET (National Science Foundation Network, the backbone of the US research Internet) wrote to Heinänen in November 1987: "If Norway, Iceland, Denmark and Sweden but not Finland were initially included, then approval could come very quickly. Finland and a number of other countries present special problems."[27] On the other hand, one reason why Finland and the other Nordic countries were able to join the TCP/IP-protocols based Internet before other European countries was that the official European position allowed only the use of OSI protocols of the International Standardization Organization (ISO) (a useful reminder of the fact that the Internet's victory in the competition for the standard for the international network of networks was by no means clear from the start. Landweber's letter to Heinänen also revealed that even the US was hesitant about the Internet: "it is the policy of the US networks to support the development of standards and the migration of our academic networks to standard (ISO) protocols when implementations are commercially available. As a corollary, we do not wish to take actions that will slow down the standards process, by, for example, promoting the development of an international TCP/IP Internet.")[28]

When the United States stopped restricting the use of the Internet to academic purposes only, Helsingius, who had been one of the initiators of the Finnish Unix User Group, established the first Finnish

[27] Landweber (1987).
[28] Landweber (1987). For the choice between TCP/IP and ISO, see Abbate (1999).

66

commercial Internet service provider, Eunet Finland, in 1993. For several years, Helsingius embodied the Internet in Finland, having an important symbolic role in Finland's shift to the Internet era (although soon the two big tele-operators, now called Sonera and Elisa, became much bigger Internet service providers). Helsingius' role could be compared to that of the famous hacker-founded XS4ALL Internet service provider in the Netherlands.[29]

*Hackers as Transformers of the Net into a Social Medium*

Finnish hackers also made an important contribution to the Net's transformation into a social medium. Helsingius represented the Internet values of free expression and privacy in a pure form and went on to create the first working anonymous remailer that made it possible to send e-mails or newsgroup messages anonymously, so that one could express sensitive views without their source being traced. Helsingius described the need for such a server thus: "Where you're dealing with minorities – racial, political, sexual, whatever – you always find cases in which people belonging to a minority would like to discuss things that are important to them without having to identify who they are."[30]

In addition to Helsingius, the strong Finnish hacker culture includes, for example, the group of young HUT students who programmed the first Web browser with graphical interface called Erwise; Tatu Ylönen, who programmed SSH encryption software; and Jarkko Oikarinen, the creator of the realtime chat or the Internet Relay Chat.

One of the main bases for Finnish hackers has been the HUT computer science department where Helsingius also studied. Every night you can find brilliant and enthusiastic programmers there, who are immersed in writing codes, remembering only in the small hours the human need for nourishment and then going together to find food or deciding to continue until breakfast time. The spirit is very close to MIT's famous AI Lab as described by Steven Levy in his *Hackers: Heroes of the Computer Revolution*.[31] Conscious of this resemblance, HUT hackers call the room where they code "MIT 2."

---

[29] Himanen (2001).     [30] Quittner (1994).     [31] Levy (1984).

## Innovation about Innovating

Ari Lemmke is one of the members of this lively culture, he is a HUT system administrator, who looks like a stereotypical hacker with his long hair and beard. In 1992, Lemmke helped a group of twenty-something students – Kim Nyberg, Teemu Rantanen, Kati Suominen, and Kari Sydänmaanlakka – to write the first mainstream operating system Web browser with a graphical interface, called Erwise.[32] They released the source code in the spring of 1992. This was a year before Mosaic and two years before Netscape. However, the students did not wish to continue the development of the software.

Tatu Ylönen was another young hacker who programmed at MIT 2.[33] He had coded there first as a student and then as a researcher. In July 1995, aged 27, Ylönen released the result of his coding, the secure shell program SSH, which encrypts network connections. Ylönen began working on the program for a combination of reasons. Earlier that winter a cracker had broken into a university system and obtained user passwords, including Ylönen's. Ylönen wanted to develop a program that would make sure this would not happen again. Security issues had intrigued him for a long time and this challenge provided a practical opportunity for learning more about cryptography (he had not formally studied the subject but became a self-taught crypto-expert by doing what he was interested in and enjoyed doing). His thinking about social values also played an important role: Ylönen was convinced that if electronic networks were not secure, someone would start to use them to monitor people or for unprecedented digital crimes. He wanted to defend the right to privacy and thus he published his program as a free software with the source code available.[34]

Tampere has been mentioned as a Finnish technology center and also with reference to the introduction of the Internet to Finland. Oulu University is the third main Finnish technology center where one of its students, Jarkko Oikarinen, began to design his real-time conversation environment or the Internet Relay Chat (IRC) (the equivalent to

---

[32] Cf. Berners-Lee (1999); Gillies and Cailliau (2000). We have obtained further information from Ari Lemmke.
[33] For the following discussion, information has been received from Tatu Ylönen.
[34] This project is currently continued by OpenSSH (see OpenSSH, 2001).

text messaging in mobile phones). The most important contribution of the IRC was the role it played in transforming the Net from the idea of shared computing resources into a new social medium. Oikarinen got his idea in the summer of 1988.[35] The Department of Information Processing Science had offered him a summer job, but as he had very little to do he started developing a new concept of a multi-server based chat environment and released the first working version by August. Initially, he did not have a very clear idea of why he was doing it: it was just born of enthusiasm for learning about socket technology, coupled with a vague idea that the software would be important for free expression (as it has proved to be, thanks to anonymity, from the messages of Kuwaitis during the Gulf War to organizing student demonstrations in Indonesia and other countries).

Soon, the HUT hackers (including Ari Lemmke) installed the software, and Tampere University of Technology quickly followed suit. This was the time that Finland had just established its first Internet link. Oikarinen used that link to access the famous MIT AI Lab ITS machine (ITS was the operating system programmed by legendary hackers like Richard Greenblatt, the system that inspired another MIT hacker Richard Stallman to start his Free Software Foundation and the GNU operating and software system development).[36] Through the link to one of the key nodes in the hacker culture, IRC started spreading rapidly. As it was an open-source program, and as Oikarinen also wrote an open standard specification for the Internet Engineering Task Force, numerous other programmers joined in its development. Nowadays, the ideas of the IRC have largely been integrated into the Web.

*Hackers as Innovators of the Open-Source Innovation Model*

Currently, the most famous Finnish hacker is undoubtedly Linus Torvalds, the creator of the Linux open-source operating system.[37]

---

[35] Oikarinen (1993); Gillies and Cailliau (2000). Some details are based on a discussion with Jarkko Oikarinen.

[36] Levy (1984); Stallman (1985, 1999); Oikarinen (1993).

[37] The following Linux model is analyzed in more detail in Himanen (2001). For histories of Linux, see Torvalds (1992*a*,*b*, 2001) and Moody (2001). Some additional information is based on discussions with Linus Torvalds.

## Innovation about Innovating

Although Torvalds continues the tradition of open development work of people like Richard Stallman and the Internet developers, he has arguably given the open-source development model a new significance by radicalizing it furthest and creating a new general innovation model.

Torvalds started to work on the operating system as a 22-year-old Helsinki University student in April 1991. He had just bought a new PC and began to experiment with its processor's features. More specifically, he studied the task-switching operation and wrote a program that switched between two tasks: one printed As and the other printed Bs. After understanding task switching, he proceeded to program the keyboard and serial port drivers to switch between these tasks and use his modem to read the newsgroups. This was the seed for an entire operating system.

On August 25, 1991, Torvalds sent to the newsgroup comp.os. minix a message saying that he was "doing a (free) operating system".[38] He received many wish lists as replies and also got some promises for beta-testers of the system. Linux 0.01 became available from the Finnish server *nic.funet.fi* in the directory /pub/OS/Linux in September 1991. The name "Linux" was given by the directory's administrator Ari Lemmke (originally Torvalds himself called the operating system "Freax" as a combination of "Freaks" and "Unix"). Version 0.02 was available from the same server at the beginning of October. After releasing this version, Torvalds made the first explicit call for others to join in the development of a new operating system. On October 5, 1991, he wrote again in *comp.os.minix*: "Do you pine for the nice days of minix-1.1, when men were men and wrote their own device drivers?" He added: "I'm also interested in hearing from anybody who has written any of the utilities/library functions for minix. If your efforts are freely distributable (under copyright or even public domain), I'd like to hear from you, so I can add them to the system."[39]

Thousands of programmers have participated in the development of Linux, not to mention the enormous number of users, which can be numbered in millions. Linux has undeniably been one of the

---

[38] Torvalds (1991*a*).     [39] Torvalds (1991*b*).

most striking recent successes in the computer world. But the most important innovation about Linux is not technical but social: it is the open-source model for developing software that Linux has taken furthest so far. The full open-source model emulates the scientific model: it starts with an individual who has a problem and publishes his or her first solution. Others who are interested in the same problem join in solving it. The openness of the model means that everyone has the right to freely use, test, and develop this solution, which is possible only if the source code is released. The openness also entails an obligation for anyone building on the open work to keep his or her work equally open (this is the idea of "copyleft – all rights reversed" deriving from Richard Stallman).[40] When this model is realized on the Internet, the result is a global network of people testing different ideas and gradually combining them into an impressive system. In practice, this type of decentralized development requires the kind of referee groups that are used in scientific publications: development is open to everyone but some people serve the community in a special role – won by their achievements and retained only as long as their choices are shared by the wider critical community – by being responsible for a certain part of the system and choosing the contributions that are incorporated in it. With consequences that still remain to be seen, in Linux Torvalds has created a new innovation model, which is slowly starting to be used for the development of software more generally and even for non-technological hackerism (as described in Chapter 4). This may prove to be one of the most radical innovations about innovating in the IT revolution.

*Hackers in the Finnish Innovation System*

To sum up, hackers are important to the Finnish innovation system in several ways. They have been the key actors in linking Finland to the Internet, they have played an important role in transforming the Net into a social medium, and they have developed the open-source innovation model. Much of this innovation has happened totally outside the business and public sectors. Linus Torvalds has become an important role model for this kind of citizen action.

---

[40]  Stallman (1999).

## Innovation about Innovating

There are some important structural reasons why this idealist form of hackerism has been so strong in Finland, although in the case of hackers it is particularly important to resist the tendency of reducing all individual action to structural factors. The main factor seems to be the Finnish educational system: the fact that universities are free and all students are entitled to a student salary plus very cheap student loans also removes short-term financial pressures. The Finnish university system also has a very high degree of academic freedom, which is supported by having no pre-prepared programs for students to follow. All of this supports and supplies a channel, for the expression of a particularly strong technology-oriented Finnish identity (as analyzed in Chapter 6).

But this does not mean that hackerism cannot relate to business. A comparison with citizen-innovated text messaging illustrates the relationship. For Nokia, the new mobile communication culture which spread as "open-source," has been very important for making mobile phones attractive. Text messaging has also generated a great income for the Finnish mobile phone operators like Sonera and Elisa, not to mention the tele-operators globally. Based on the widespread mobile culture, many Finnish TV channels now make money by broadcasting moderated text-messaging chats for hours after their regular programming, something that may spread to other countries with rising mobile phone penetration. In a similar way, hackers have created business. Helsingius is an example of a hacker as a start-up entrepreneur, and Heinänen is an example of a hacker as a driving force within a large corporation as he moved to work for Sonera and later for Telia.

And although Torvalds himself has not turned Linux into a business, it does not mean that there cannot be open-source business. Many companies have been started on the open-source model both in Finland and elsewhere. There are Linux companies, such as the Finnish SOT (distributing Best Linux) or the American Red Hat, whose business models are based on selling services. Big companies like Nokia have started to use the open-source model for developing mobile phone software, based on the business model that their real income comes from elsewhere. American companies like IBM have adopted Linux and invested in its development, based on the idea of making an income by selling machines running the operating system.

If one wants to note a downside of the Finnish hacker spirit, however, from the point of view of business innovation, the fate of Erwise is a good example: the students did not fully understand the opportunity they had created and they stopped the development of the browser, leaving the opportunity for the later web revolution to Mosaic and Netscape. On the other hand, from their perspective, this was no great loss as they were not motivated by money in the first place. They preferred new technical challenges and went on to new projects. The hacker ethos, which reminds us that there are other values besides money, is an important balancing force for the spirit of the new economy and gives Finland a different social tone from Silicon Valley.

## The Finnish Innovation System

Finally, let us sum up the various elements of the Finnish innovation system and its development. As is well known, the real fruits of the Finnish innovation system were reaped only after the recession at the beginning of the 1990s. This was the time when Nokia grew into a global leader in mobile telecommunications, and helped other Finnish telecommunications companies like Sonera and Elisa and electronics manufacturing service companies like Elcoteq to follow its international path, encouraging new IT companies to sprout in Finland. The recession meant "creative destruction," making companies like Nokia restructure themselves even more radically than they might have done under other circumstances.

However, it would be wrong to claim that the rise of Finnish information technology was just a result of the recession, and even more wrong to think that Finnish information-society strategies written since 1994 have been its main source. The eventual success of Finnish IT has been the result of a quarter-century of technology policy. If the most decisive moment is to be dated, then the best candidates are the events of the early 1980s consisting of the government's decision-in-principle to raise research and development investment and carry out this project systematically, including in particular the establishment of the Science and Technology Policy Council and Tekes. Finnish IT growth had

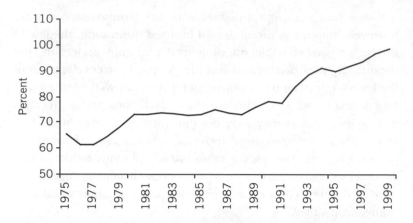

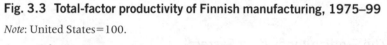

**Fig. 3.3 Total-factor productivity of Finnish manufacturing, 1975–99**

*Note*: United States=100.

*Source*: Etla.

already begun by the late 1980s with productivity going up significantly, which could be interpreted as a delayed consequence of the early 1980s' action, as it is known that the influence of research and development investments becomes visible after a delay of a few years (see Fig. 3.3).

However, this growth was immediately hit by the recession. The reasons for the recession are discussed in more detail in Chapter 4, but briefly put, the recession can be characterized as Finland's teething troubles in the course of joining the global informational economy. An additional reason why the results of the Finnish innovation system had to wait until after the recession is that this was a global phenomenon. The IT revolution, which began in the last quarter of the twentieth century, accelerated in 1994 with the massive breakthrough of the Internet. The growth in the stock value of the Finnish IT companies – as well as the rise of the Finnish hackers – must be understood in this global context.

To sum up, one can say that the key elements of the Finnish innovation system, which has evolved over a quarter of a century and ultimately turned the economy round after the recession, are:

1. *An active public policy of innovation* based on high investment in research and development under the guidance of the Science and Technology Policy Council. A public, free, high-quality university

system, which has a strong emphasis on engineering, creates the human basis for innovation (basic research innovations, employees for the companies, and hackers). The technology research and development financer Tekes and the "public capitalist" Sitra provide financial support for risky corporate innovation. And the liberalization, deregulation, and privatization policy, combined with *avant-garde* thinking about open standards, creates a positive culture of innovation. Contingent political reasons have had their input, but they were not the key reasons for success.

2. *Business innovation*, which is encouraged by public action but which is ultimately based on the company's ability to recruit, keep, and use its talented R&D people, providing the necessary financial basis for turning innovations into products through market mechanisms, and a company culture of innovation.

3. *Hacker innovation*, which is driven by talented individuals, who are often supported by public systems such as free universities and student grants, and has the hacker ethic as its innovation culture. Hackers relate to business through the companies they found or are hired by, as well as through the adoption of their innovations, such as the open-source model, by corporations. (The case of citizen innovation is similar to this: corporations adopted citizen-innovated text messaging and made it into a business.)

Although some factors can be singled out as more important than others, the decisive point about the Finnish innovation system is the combination of the above factors – its holistic approach. The Finnish innovation system is not a list of factors but a unique network of interactions. The networking tendency of the Finnish innovation system, which combines all of its components, is so central that the continued networking of various parties should be spelled out as an underlying driving factor. There are important national identity elements that shape the special nature of and reasons for Finnish networking; because of its significance this factor will be discussed separately in Chapter 6. But here it can be noted that there is clearly something very important in the high level of networking between companies, the government, universities, and hackers. For example, according to the second European Community Innovation Survey, 53 percent of

## Innovation about Innovating

Finnish innovative companies had cooperation agreements with universities in 1994–6, compared with an EU average of 7.5 percent. According to an OECD study, Finland is the second in its country group, measured by the share of companies having cooperation agreements with universities or public research institutions.[41] In addition to their specific technological results, an important outcome of the large number of committees, councils, steering groups, forums, and so on that have been established by the Finnish government has been the networking of people in industry, universities, and the government. The key people are very highly networked personally, as they meet with each other constantly in various groups and at social events. In the Finnish IT cluster, "Everybody knows everybody."

This networking has created a kind of Silicon Valley effect where ideas are exchanged and people take their knowledge from one environment to another.[42] However, the degree of public-sector involvement differentiates these forms of networking from each other. To put it a little playfully, in Silicon Valley entrepreneurs met in the famous Walker's Wagon Wheel Bar and Grill; in Finland, the government provides the coffee and muffins so that people can network. Except, of course, for the hackers who prefer to drink coke and just do what they believe in and network with other like-minded individuals.

---

[41] OECD (1999).     [42] Cf. Saxenian (1994).

Chapter 4

# THE WELFARE OF THE NATION
## The Information Society and the Welfare State

Despite its centrality, the informational economy, with the techno-economic innovations that are behind it, forms only one dimension of the network society. For citizens, the decisive question is: what kind of social dimension is this techno-economic development combined with? We will discuss the relationship between identity and the network society in Chapter 6. At the level of social justice, the dominant global trend is that the network society connects to itself those people who are valuable to it (and creates further value for them) and disconnects those who are valueless to it (and decreases further their ability to acquire value). The result is growing social injustice.[1] For example, income inequality is increasing in most advanced countries

[1] Cf. Castells (2000a).

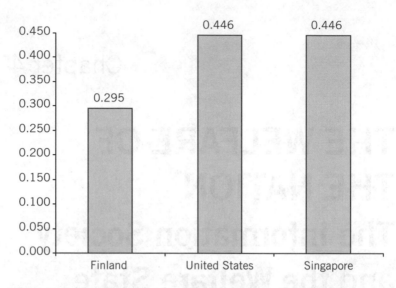

**Fig. 4.1 Social injustice measured by the Gini index, 1998**

*Note*: The figures are based on the gross income Gini index (for an explanation of the Gini index, see the note to Fig. 1.5 in Chapter 1).

*Sources*: The figure for Finland is based on Riihelä and Sullström (2001); the figure for the United States is based on the US Census Bureau (1999); the figure for Singapore is based on the Singapore Department of Statistics (2001).

and is now at a very high level. Figure 1.3 in Chapter 1 showed that in Silicon Valley and Singapore the income of the richest fifth of the population is approximately ten times the income of the poorest fifth. In Finland, the figure is roughly one-third of this level. The same difference between the global trend and the Finnish model is shown in the Gini indexes compared in Fig. 4.1.

The global trend is a result of the decline of the welfare state, whose task it was to guarantee social justice through education, health care, and income transfers. Social injustice leads in its extreme form to social exclusion, in which a person left living in misery cannot change his or her fate without, perhaps, choosing crime as a means of survival. Social exclusion is difficult to measure, but the commonly used incarceration rate gives some indication of the scale of exclusion (see Fig. 4.2).

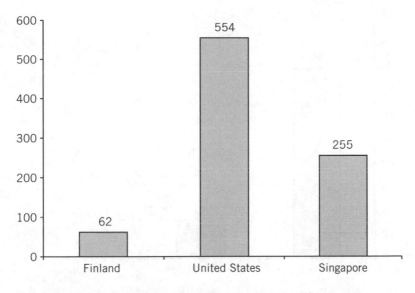

**Fig. 4.2** Social exclusion measured by the incarceration rate per
100 000 population, 2000

*Source*: UNDP (2000).

As different types of exclusion are on the rise, the global trend has
also brought into question the idea of inclusive development, which
was the task of the welfare state.

In addition to social justice, the wider concept of the welfare state
included the collective protection of the labor force. The information
economy has also weakened this dimension because it has introduced
the concept of the informational labor force, which does not refer only
to IT skills and the centrality of information (symbol) processing, but
also to the organization of labor as a network: labor is arranged around
companies as a network from which people are connected and dis-
connected, according to the varying needs of projects, on a temporary,
part-time, and self-employment basis.[2] This results in individualized
contracts and very low levels of labor unionization globally (see Fig. 4.3).
Thus, the welfare state idea of guaranteeing the rights of labor through
contracts between the state, employers, and employees is becoming
an exception rather than the rule.

[2] Cf. Castells (2000*a*).

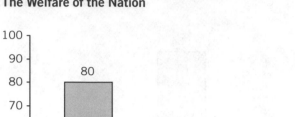

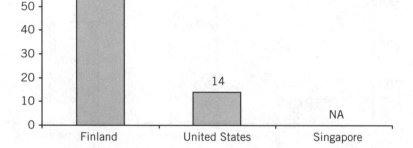

**Fig. 4.3 The collective protection of labor measured by the rate of unionization (percent), 1996**

*Source*: Bratt (1996).

The demise of the welfare state can be expressed not only in these observable trends but also in what cannot be observed: there is a widespread impression that informationalism and the welfare state are antagonistic, although there has been no serious discussion about how informationalism and the welfare state could be combined. However, the notion of an informational welfare state is possible. Its core is a virtuous circle in which the informational economy and the welfare state feed into each other, including the traditional elements of social justice and the collective protection of labor. But a fully "informational" welfare state would also be something new. The informationalization of the welfare state also means applying information technology to welfare purposes and renewing the structures of the welfare state through a more dynamic network organization. This type of innovation increases the productivity of the public services and relieves the financial pressures on the welfare state.

These challenges have become more and more important in the present context of the social contradictions related to increasing social injustice and social exclusion. Against this global background, the universally most challenging part of the Finnish model is that it gives us an example of what the informational welfare state could be like in practice.

## The Information Society and the Welfare State

The main elements of the Finnish welfare state have been free education (no fees from pre-school to university and free school books and meals until high school, plus a student grant for further education), very cheap health services (mainly free health centers, low-priced hospitals, subsidized drugs, home-care support), and social protection through income transfers (retirement insurance, sickness insurance, disability insurance, unemployment insurance, child-care support, and income support). As well as being free, a key characteristic of the system has been its universality: welfare rights are based on citizenship (or, lately, residence) and thus the level of welfare benefits that a person is entitled to does not primarily depend on his or her income (although income and need are taken into account). The third distinctive feature is the highly public nature of the system: most welfare services are provided publicly (e.g., virtually all schools and 76 percent of health expenditure are public). Or, to put it in the familiar terms of the welfare-state researchers, the Finnish welfare-state model is institutional[3] and "social democratic."[4]

This is the system behind the low levels of social injustice and exclusion in Finland. However, before concluding that a different Finnish model of the information society really does exist, let us face a serious question. It could be argued that the Finnish combination of an information society and a welfare state is ultimately an optical illusion, hiding the fact that the information society is rising while the welfare state is beginning to fade away. In this case, we could just be witnessing the last moment of the overlapping of two very different trends. It

[3] As distinct from earnings-related or residual; see Wilensky and Lebeaux (1958); Titmuss (1968, 1974).
[4] As distinct from conservative and liberal welfare regimes; see Esping-Andersen (1990).

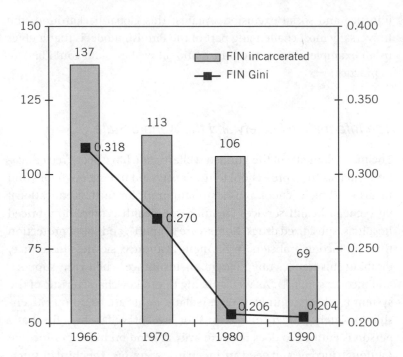

**Fig. 4.4  Social injustice and exclusion in the shift from an industrial to a network society in Finland, 1966–90**

*Sources*: The Gini figures are based on Deininger and Squire (1996); Riihelä and Sullström (2001). The incarceration figures are based on von Hofer (1997).

is critical to judge which is the case. We can start to approach the answer by analyzing another version of a diagram presented in Chapter 1 (Fig. 4.4; cf. Fig. 1.5).

The time perspective of the rise of the information society from the 1970s onward is important for a full understanding of the trend in the Finnish welfare state. Figure 4.4 gives strong evidence to show that the general trend in Finnish social injustice and exclusion was downward, or at least remained at a low level, during the main years of the rise of the information society between 1966 and 1990. As shown in Chapter 1, this is in sharp contrast to the United States where the shift from an industrial to an information society reversed the trends and has set both social injustice and exclusion at very high levels.

However, this important observation is not enough. As the Finnish economy was mainly growing between 1966 and 1990, the recession in 1990–3 must be seen as the biggest test of the Finnish welfare state. The recession was also related to the shift to the global informational economy. It was caused by a combination of the partial failure of the liberalization of financial markets (the critical moment for the formation of global financial markets), which made both companies and individuals take on debts based on inflated real-estate values; and the simultaneous downturn of the Western economies (another crisis of capitalism that they overcame) along with the collapse of the Soviet Union (because of the failure of communism in adapting to informationalism), which were the major markets for Finland. Measured by GDP and employment, Finland's recession in 1990–3 was deeper than in any other industrial country. The GDP decreased by 13 percent and the unemployment rate went up from 3.5 to 17 percent in 1994 (see Fig. 4.5).

What did this deep recession do to the Finnish welfare state? Because of the importance of the question, the Finnish Academy began a major research program in 1998 called "The Economic Crisis of the 1990s," involving more than one hundred experts from different fields, to focus on the impact of the recession. The program concluded in the fall of 2001. Based on an extensive analysis of the empirical data, the research program's main conclusion (for the purposes of this book) is that – in spite of significant cuts in social and health expenditure and the introduction of stricter controls on the use of services – the main educational, health, and social service components of the Finnish welfare state remain fundamentally unchanged.[5] The Finnish welfare state continues to be based on the public school system, universal health insurance, non-employment related retirement insurance, and so on.

However, the research program also emphasizes some worrying developments. For example, home care for the elderly, psychiatric care, and help for substance abusers – also components of the traditional welfare state – were cut significantly. Moreover, the research program presents evidence that there was some increase in income

[5] Simpura *et al.* (2001).

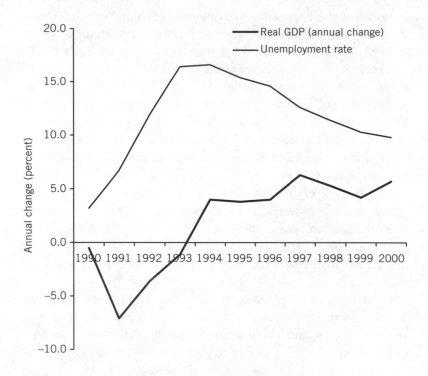

**Fig. 4.5 The GDP and the unemployment rate, 1990–2000**

inequality in the last years of the 1990s, attributable to the combination of the long-term unemployment of the poorest and the capital income of the richest.[6] It emphasizes that there is no evidence for the formation of an underclass of the excluded, but the observation of a rise in income inequality is already significant; in fact, it forms a challenge that will be discussed separately in Chapter 8.

Of course, here the critical question is: what is the scale of the impact of the recession on the Finnish welfare state? For the moment,

[6] See Kalela *et al.* (2001), especially Kangasharju *et al.* (2001), Riihelä *et al.* (2001), and Ritakallio (2001).

even using the stocks/options gains peak year of 1998 (the last for which published data are available) as our reference point, the Finnish Gini index of 0.245 is still in the same class as it was in 1990 (0.200–0.250). In addition, whereas in the United States the 1998 Gini index of 0.419 was significantly higher than in the late 1960s, before the advent of the information society, in Finland the 1998 Gini index of 0.245 was considerably lower than the pre-information society Gini index of 0.318 in 1966.[7] Finland's figure continues to be one of the world's lowest Gini indexes, and thus the distinctiveness of the Finnish model has remained, as Kautto et al. have shown in their comparative study.[8] Thus, so far, the evidence supports the conclusion that, in spite of the pressures of the global information economy, Finland continues to be a different form of an information society, which combines with it a generous welfare state.

## Collective Labor Protection

Another traditional aspect of the welfare state has been the collective protection of the labor force; in fact, labor unions have been a major historical source of the welfare state. Thus, the global demise of the welfare state is linked to the decreasing collective protection of the labor force, and there is a widespread impression that informational work and labor unionization are even mutually exclusive. This means that the old social contract between labor, capital, and the state is disappearing and is not being replaced by a new social contract.

It is important to understand the Finnish case in this context. In Finland, labor unions have been especially central actors in the welfare state. The labor unions do not just look after the interests of their working members, but they are also an important social security net for the unemployed through their sizable unemployment insurance. The difference from the global trend is that, in the 1990s, about 80 percent of the Finnish labor force remained unionized (compared with 14 percent in the United States).[9] The Finnish system of industrial

---

[7] Deininger and Squire (1996); US Census Bureau (1999); and Riihelä and Sullström (2001).     [8] Kautto et al. (2001).
[9] Bratt (1996).

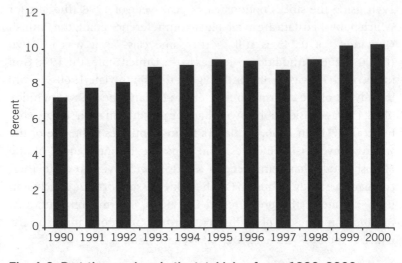

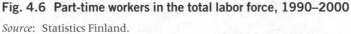

Fig. 4.6  Part-time workers in the total labor force, 1990–2000

*Source*: Statistics Finland.

relations, characterized by the system of annual collective bargaining between employee and employer organizations and the government, still continues to function.

At the same time, the strong role of the labor unions has not acted as a block to the new informational work that the economy needs. Statistics Finland has analyzed for our use the development of flexible work (self-employment, temporary work, part-time work) in Finland during the most visible years of the rise of the information society (1990–2000). The full data are given in Appendix 1. The main observation from the analysis is that the share of flexible work in Finland in 2000 was relatively high at 37.7 percent of all jobs. During the past decade, the share of flexible work also grew considerably. Because of the change in classification, the best available indicator of growth is the share of part-time workers, which increased by 41 percent between 1990 and 2000, as shown in Fig. 4.6.

Thus, the Finnish model differs from the global trend: it combines informational work (including new flexibility) with the collective protection of labor. It seems that this has been made possible through a two-directional process: by allowing the new flexibility needed in the informational economy, the labor unions (the welfare state) have kept their role as a contemporary negotiating partner with capital; while the welfare state – including its comprehensive coverage of social benefits regardless of employment situation – has made it less difficult for labor to accept the new flexibility of the information economy.

However, there is also a surprising observation about flexible work in the Statistics Finland data. Although the share of flexible work grew faster in the IT sector than in the total labor force (67 percent measured by the available indicator of the share of part-time workers), it remained at 18.8 percent in 2000. This is in line with the general rise of flexible work in the informational economy, but it is rather unexpected that the flexibility is lower in the IT field, which drives the development. An important challenge that arises from this situation will be discussed in Chapter 8.

## The Informational Welfare State

Thus, empirical observations support the conclusion that the Finnish model combines a dynamic informational economy with stronger social justice and a collective protection of labor – the old tasks of the welfare state – than the global trend. However, it is no longer the old species of welfare state, which was often just seen as the alleviator of the economy's worst effects and occupied a fundamentally defensive position against the economy. At the beginning of this chapter, we proposed the concept of the "informational welfare state" to describe a welfare state that forms a virtuous circle with the informational economy.

There are several important links between them. First, the Finnish information society creates the financial basis for the welfare state. Without tax income, society could not finance its welfare state. And without increased productivity, taxes would be too high to be acceptable to people. The information society therefore needs to grow faster than the costs of the welfare state. Figure 4.7 shows how this has been achieved in Finland.

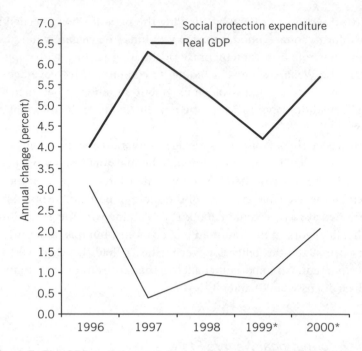

**Fig. 4.7 The GDP and the social expenditure growth, 1996–2000**

*Note*: The * indicates an estimate.

The competitive productivity of the economy is also necessary to keep companies in the country. There can be higher labor and social costs only if there is higher productivity; otherwise, companies will relocate to places with a lower level of taxation. So, at a basic level, the informational economy and the welfare state are not antagonistic, but a successful informational economy is a requirement for a gener-ous welfare state. It is only through the transformation of its economy that Finland could continue as a welfare state even through a severe recession.

But, in the long run, the informational economy needs to have a sustainable social dimension. In fact, the idea of the informational economy as a prerequisite of the welfare state could be presented the other way round: in view of the current strong opposition to global-ization, it could be that, without a stronger global welfare dimension,

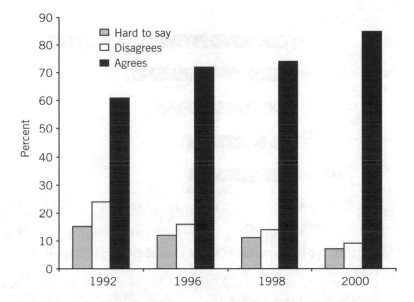

Fig. 4.8  Finnish attitudes toward the welfare state. "Even if good social security and other public services are expensive they are worth it"

*Source*: EVA (2001).

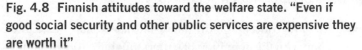

the informational economy may face such harsh opposition that its development will become extremely volatile or be unable to continue. This would make some type of welfare state a prerequisite for the global informational economy. Seen from this perspective, Finland was able to continue its transformation into an informational economy during the recession because the welfare state made the development socially acceptable. Of course, another key reverse link is that it is the public provision of education, health, and social security that ensures a sufficient number of highly educated people in good shape to work in the informational economy. As a result of this virtuous circle, Finns continue to support the welfare state very strongly (Figs 4.8 and 4.9).

So what we are seeing in the Finnish model is a new informational welfare state. The core is the virtuous circle of the informational economy and the welfare state.

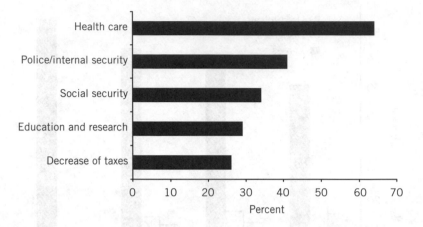

Fig. 4.9 The top five priorities of Finns in relation to public services

## Social Uses of Information Technology

However, the full concept of the *informational* welfare state also includes, in line with the definition of "informational," the social uses of information technology and the renewal of the welfare state structure through a more dynamic network organization. Let us see how far the Finnish model has progressed in these two respects. The main source for the development of social uses of information technology is the Finnish information-society strategies. The first national information-society strategy was written in the context of the recession of 1993–4 and thus it very much emphasized economy and technology.[10] However, the most important part of the strategy comprised the new social goals that it set (the key economic and technological ideas about technology innovation and cluster had already been

---

[10] The strategy states on its opening page: "The need for renewal stems primarily from three sources: Finland's economy merging with an open and changing world economy, mass unemployment and the setback experienced by our national economy and pressures for change posed by new technologies" (Ministry of Finance, 1995). We have also received information on the strategy's background from Esko Aho, Prime Minister of Finland, and Tauno Heikkilä, the secretary of the group that wrote the strategy.

introduced by the Science and Technology Policy Council and enjoyed a wide support, as described in Chapter 3).[11]

Prime Minister Esko Aho's government confirmed the strategy's goals in its decision-in-principle on the information society in January 1995. The strategy and its confirmation by government include, for example, the following welfare state goals:[12]

- networking of all educational institutions and libraries
- the use of information technology in education (including the experiment of a virtual university)
- net literacy
- uses of information technology for the elderly
- formation of a well-being cluster.

When Paavo Lipponen's government came to power in April 1995, it included essentially the same goals in its government program.[13] These goals were also explicated in the separate strategies of each ministry, especially the Ministry of Education and the Ministry of Social Affairs and Health.[14]

The first strategy phase lasted from 1995–8 when the second general information-society strategy was written.[15] The 1998 strategy had an even stronger social tone than the 1994 strategy: it hardly mentioned the economy and technology and instead focused predominantly on welfare goals.[16] Based on the first strategy's proposals, an Information Society Forum of some fifty experts was formed to develop ideas for the Information Society Committee, which was established as the government's advisory board on information-society matters (the committee consisted of ten representatives of

[11] Thus, it was natural for the council's 1996 review to reformulate its earlier ideas in the vocabulary of the information society.

[12] Council of State (1995*a*); Ministry of Finance (1995).

[13] Council of State (1995*b*). The same goals were also included in the Government's Future Report to Parliament in 1997 (Council of State, 1997) and Parliament gave its strong support to them in its Reply to the Government's Future Report (Parliament of Finland Committee for the Future, 1998*a*).

[14] Ministry of Education (1995); Ministry of Social Affairs and Health (1996).

[15] For general evaluations of the implementation of the first information strategy, see Ministry of Finance (1996) and Lilius (1997).

[16] Sitra (1998).

companies, universities, and the government). These two groups suggested the writing of a second version of the strategy, which was then largely organized by Sitra, as described in Chapter 3. The actual drafting process took place from 1997–8. The resulting updated strategies by ministries in 1999–2000 were much more specific than those of 1995.[17] Again, Lipponen's second government included most of these goals in its government program in 1999.[18] During 1999, development networks were organized for each goal, in line with the strategy's proposal. Sitra also provided a forum for the projects to network directly with each other in its Spearhead Project Network.[19]

*Health*

Health provision is one of the foundations of the welfare state. New information technology can provide many new opportunities in the health field. This was recognized in the first national information-society strategy and more comprehensively in the strategy of the Ministry of Social Affairs and Health in 1996.[20]

Stakes, the Welfare Research and Development Agency, a relatively autonomous institution under the ministry, has been an especially active participant in the ideation of health applications of information technology. Since 1994, Stakes has advanced the idea of a well-being cluster led by its director Vappu Taipale, one of Finland's most visible female visionaries of the information society.[21] The most interesting and newest emphasis of Stakes has been the use of technology for the old in its *Senior 2000* report.[22] The background is that Finland's population is aging fast. Unless migration or war changes the trends, in 2030, people over the age of 65 will comprise more than a quarter of the population and fewer than every sixth person will be under 15 (in 1950, the corresponding figures were: every fifteenth person over 65 and almost a third of the population under 15).[23]

---

[17] Ministry of Education (1999*a,b*, 2001).     [18] Council of State (1999).
[19] Cf. *http://karkiverkosto.sitra.fi.*
[20] Ministry of Social Affairs and Health (1996). The first strategy (Ministry of Finance, 1995) contains a separate section on the welfare society applications in its Appendix 1 (Kajander *et al.*, 1994).     [21] Taipale (1994).
[22] Sonkin *et al.* (1999).     [23] Sonkin *et al.* (1999).

Future pensioners will be very different from earlier generations. The new seniors are not so much patients as customers, not people who just need to be supported, but wealthy consumers; instead of remaining passive, they want to be active. There is a great need for technology to support independent living, based on the idea of being able to remain in one's own home until the end of one's life, and to access services and social networks on par with adults in full health.

The report also makes new suggestions to facilitate mobility. For example, city planning should take traffic more seriously, starting with traffic lights that could gauge a pedestrian's speed and allow the time they need to cross the street. There could be solutions that would complement walking, such as hill lifts to enable seniors to climb up the steeper hills, and heated paths to make it possible for the elderly to be out in winter. The report even mentions the possibility of new senior city vehicles called "three-wheeled Harley Davidsons."

These ideas of gerontechnology are recognized more and more widely and they have been developed in concrete projects by Stakes. For example, in 1995, Stakes started a well-being cluster program in Oulu,[24] and in 1998 it was central in the decision of the Ministry of Social Affairs and Health to start an ambitious well-being cluster project called Macro Pilot, which has grown into the biggest endeavor of its kind in Europe.[25]

The Macro Pilot includes subprojects on the technology of independent living, such as an advanced home-caring system in which patients, who would normally have to remain in hospital, can be cared for at home (with the help of technology their state of health can be monitored 24 h a day). However, so far the project has come closest to its goals in the creation of a seamless health-care system, in which the customer does not have to be concerned with the boundaries between different organizations; all needs are served through one service point. The idea is to eliminate all unnecessary "running around" (e.g., if an additional expertise is needed, the health-care worker makes a virtual connection to the expert instead of referring the customer in person) and superfluous movements of paper (e.g., the project includes

---

[24] Koivukangas and Valtonen (1995*a,b*); Stakes (1997).
[25] *www.makropilotti.fi*.

electronic prescriptions). The project uses a new electronic ID card to allow electronic identification, with an emphasis on security and privacy. With the customer's permission, medical information about him or her will be saved in a database that is open to doctors and pharmacists, to help in medical decisions. The Macro Pilot has managed to advance cooperation between public bodies considerably and it has brought together many innovative companies, like Welfare Communications that develops seamless solutions, and OuluTech, a seedbed for health-technology companies. The project has just completed its plan for disseminating its results in order to transform the national health system at large.[26]

There are now signs that a new well-being cluster is forming in Finland. The potential of this cluster was noted as early as the beginning of the 1990s in Etla's cluster research.[27] The idea is, of course, based on the belief that Finland has special strength both in IT and welfare services and that their combination would be something exceptional on a global scale. Stakes took the initiative in starting the idea's actualization, but the Ministry of Social Affairs and Health, the Ministry of Trade and Industry, Tekes (through its technology programs called Digital Media in Health Care and I-Well), Sitra (through its venture capital investments), and the Finnish Academy (Research Project on Aging) have joined in its implementation.[28]

*Education*

By its nature, the other foundation of the welfare state, education, also provides many opportunities for the use of information technology. Knowledge and information technology go together. In strategies, the educational goal that has been reached fastest and most

---

[26] The Ministry of Social Affairs and Health (2001).

[27] The welfare-related reports of Etla include Rouvinen *et al.* (1995) and Mäkinen *et al.* (1999). For a very brief history of the well-being cluster, see Saranummi (1999). In addition to the activities of the Ministry of Social Affairs and Health, the Ministry of Trade and Industry also started its well-being cluster program in 1995.

[28] Some of the network's current communication is contained in the Network of Welfare Excellence Centers, *www.oskenet.fi*.

completely is the networking of the whole educational system and libraries, which took place with a special funding from the Ministry of Education.[29]

The implementation of other goals has proceeded more slowly but with increased consensus about their significance. The second educational strategy shifted the emphasis even more clearly from the technological infrastructure to its educational uses and formulated a systematic approach. The new strategy contains – in addition to the program called Structures of the Information Society, which continues the building of the necessary infrastructure – seven other programs: Information Society Skills (Net literacy), Education for Teachers (Net pedagogical skills), Education for Information Professionals (engineers etc.), Virtual University (a virtual learning environment for the tertiary level), Virtual School (a virtual learning environment for primary and secondary levels), Virtual Learning Environments (the development of new general learning environments based on modern pedagogy), and Content Production (organized under the Ministry of Culture).[30]

Of these, the furthest in practice is the Virtual School, which offers the most high school courses on the Net.[31] The Virtual University was offi cially founded at the beginning of 2001 as a cooperative effort between all twenty Finnish universities, but it is still very much under development.[32] By themselves, the Virtual School and the Virtual University do not make Finland an especially advanced country in the educational applications of information technology, but if one adds the numerous corporate learning applications and some general virtual learning environments there is reason to say that Finland has a lot of potential in this area. The main problem is the making of products out of projects rather than the lack of expertise or good development work – a problem that is currently being tackled with an e-learning cluster initiative.

---

[29] The implementation of the educational goals has been studied particularly extensively both from the initiative of the ministry itself – Ministry of Education (1997) and Nevgi (2000) – and as a result of a joint research project of the Parliament of Finland Committee for the Future and Sitra. See Hein (1998); Huovinen (1998); Lehtiö (1998); Viteli (1998); Viteli *et al.* (1998); Sinko and Lehtinen (1999); and the Parliament of Finland Committee for the Future (1998*a*, 1999*a*).

[30] See *www.minedu.fi/opm/hankkeet/sisu/index.html.*

[31] *www.oph.fi/etalukio.*        [32] *www.virtuaaliyliopisto.fi.*

Oddly, despite its high position in the strategies, the advancement of Net literacy still depends mainly on individual projects and has not been integrated systematically into the school and university curriculums or offered on a wide basis to the adult population. This may be changing because of the new Information Skills program,[33] but so far the most interesting Net literacy project has not originated from the strategies of the government or corporations but has been citizen-based.

## Social Hackerism

The role of citizens in the Finnish welfare state is comparable to their role in the Finnish innovation system; neither dimension consists solely of the public and private sectors. We can talk about "social hackerism" as an expression of the welfare state through civil society and applying the hacker model of sharing resources to some social goal instead of software. In Finland, social hackerism has had an important role to play where the strategies of government have been unimaginative or slow to be realized and where commercial interest has been lacking. Let us elaborate what we mean by social hackerism with three examples.[34]

*Sharing Time*

Net literacy is a good example of applying the hacker model of sharing in a new way. In Net literacy, the biggest problem is, of course, not young children but the adult population. To tackle this problem, a project was developed called "Learn about your Child's Future."[35] The main person behind the concept was Veli-Antti Savolainen, a father of two children and an enthusiast for school–home cooperation, who suggested that children could act as "agents" in the advancement of Net literacy. He organized a voluntary group of school teachers with Net skills, who gave their 11-year-old pupils an invitation to their

---

[33] The Ministry of Education Information Skills Working Group (2000).
[34] This idea is introduced by Himanen (2001).
[35] *www.huominen.net.* Additional information has been received from Veli-Antti Savolainen.

parents (sometimes also to neighbors and grandparents) to come to school to learn the skills of the network society. The message in the letter of invitation that the children brought home was: "Do you want to come and learn about my future?" It was not surprising that only a few parents responded by saying "No, I don't care about your future."

Savolainen was able to gain support for the project from the Ministry of Education, especially for the production of the Net literacy ABC book. Also, the Association of Local and Regional Authorities (Kuntaliitto), the Teachers' Professional Association (OAJ), and several universities helped in the process. The National Broadcasting Company participated by broadcasting a TV training course (which was also distributed as a video to the learning groups). However, the project was largely implemented without public support; for example, Sitra was not interested in financing it.

The first step in getting the adults into school was a series of events organized throughout Finland for teachers. Their main purpose was to encourage teachers to join in the idea. Everything happened on a voluntary basis. Enthusiastic teachers started learning groups in their schools. Sometimes a parent who was an expert in computers joined the teachers in training others. Many times pupils from the class taught their own and also their classmates' parents. It was a case of sharing resources by giving one's time. The courses were not just about technical skills but also about the challenges of the informational economy and what they mean for all of us. The courses also discussed the social dimension of the information society, which resulted in many social effects. In fact, the social networking of parents with schools and with each other was as important as the technical skills learned, although this networking was again helped by the Net-based environment (a publishing/learning system, which included e-mail addresses for everyone), which made continued interaction possible. Many of these parents were, of course, decision-makers in enterprises and the public sector and when they saw the reality of information technology in schools, they often helped the schools to make improvements.

After its first phase, the project began to involve trainers from other organizations. It also formed more focused subprojects, like teaching

Net literacy skills systematically in a municipality (with the backing of the local authorities, as in Lempäälä) or in some professional group (with the backing of the workers' union as in the case of the Union of Health and Social Care Professionals, Tehy). In total, tens of thousands of adults have participated in the courses, giving rise, in their turn, to new ideas of social hackerism: for example, some parents decided to start a Net-based neighborhood day-care circle in which people can share their time for child care (non-virtually). Another important idea of sharing time has been social hackerism in the labor movement: as the system gives *all* members of the labor union an e-mail address through which they can be collectively reached immediately, the idea is that the Net can become a powerful mobilizer of informational labor strikes. Just let everyone know the time and place for a strike and you have a "demonstration by click."

*Sharing Learning*

Further examples of applying the hacker model of sharing to a social goal are the open-source learning environments that have been created by individuals who were frustrated with the slow progress of the official virtual university. One of these softwares is called the FLE, which is developed by sharing code, just like in the Linux movement. But there is also a larger project called Academeia starting with the objective of expanding the computer hacker approach from the tools of learning to the content and process of learning itself.[36]

This project's important background observation is that what distinguishes the 12-year-old computer hacker, who can learn extremely complex matters, from other kids who learn very slowly in schools is not that he or she would be radically smarter than his or her contemporaries. The biggest difference is three other factors in their relation to learning: First, computer hackers are passionate about programming. They are extremely curious about the world of programming and want to understand more and more about it. Second, because of their passionate approach to learning, computer hackers take an active role: they set their own questions and problems and build their

---

[36] For a more extensive analysis, see Himanen (2001: ch. 4). For updated information about the project, see www.hackerethic.org.

own solutions by using, and critically evaluating, different sources of information from books to the Net. And, third, they are not isolated learners but share their learning process: they belong to a community of computer hackers, which includes both novices and more advanced hackers, from whom they can both get and give help. In addition, the "learning materials" are put together by the learners. When a hacker learns something, he or she often writes about it for others. Then new learners use this knowledge, correct errors in it, and develop it further. Thus, the learning of computer hackers also teaches others and the learning materials accumulate through each learner. The reward is peer recognition.

This model is naturally very close to how academic learning takes place. Researchers also have a passionate, problem-based and shared learning process. The idea of Academeia is to apply this learning model, which has proved to be powerful both in the history of science and in computer hackerism, to learning in general. In this model, learners build the collective learning materials, with teachers encouraging their innate curiosity and capabilities of learning to learn. The teachers adopt the same role as in the old Socratic philosophy of learning that was behind Plato's Academy, the first "university" in the world: they are the midwives, the gadflies and the symposiarchs of learning. If this open-source process of cumulative building of Academeia really takes flight, it can become – like the Net literacy concept – especially important for the less-developed countries of the world by providing open access to the best learning on the Net.

*Sharing Information*

The third example of social hackerism that we want to discuss is the sharing of information. Through this example we also want to link the concept of social hackerism more precisely to the concept of computer hackerism. Computer hackerism starts with an individual who has a great idea and some personal resources. Then, this individual announces his or her idea to others. Those who believe in the same vision join in the realization of the vision by contributing complementary resources. The development can be open to varying degrees; the open-source model's idea of giving one's resources totally and openly for anyone to use, test, and to develop further being the most radical one. In all cases, the direct individual-to-individual action forms a powerful network that can accomplish very big things, as in the case of Linux.

In social hackerism, the shared resource is not a source code but something that advances a social goal. But, although social hackerism is organized through the Net, it is not limited to virtual reality. Above, we saw that in the idea of sharing time, something takes place in physical reality; for example, child care or a labor demonstration. The sharing of learning also has implications on the organization of the physical learning environment.

Our third example also has a physical dimension. The sharing of information is very important for different kinds of citizen organizations with ethical goals. We take vegetarianism as an example because here we have an especially good instance of using the open-source model for something other than software in an actual up and running project. In vegetarianism (and eating in general), recipes are the source code. The problem of everyday vegetarianism is the same as in many other ethical movements: the history of mankind has put its energy into perfecting other forms of existence so there is a need for a rapid development process in an underdeveloped area. In more concrete terms, this means that, while meat cuisine has been perfected and thus meat-eating is very easy in practice, vegetarian cuisine is totally underdeveloped and thus a very difficult choice. To solve this problem, a site *www.vegetariangourmet.org* has been started to develop good vegetarian food through a Linux-like process of open sharing of information: all recipes are totally open for anyone to use, test, and develop further. The development is even modularized like the Linux development: competing groups focusing on imitation chicken, and so on are forming. It will be interesting to see what other ethical projects start in this area of sharing information, where one can immediately see many applications in developing countries.

## Informational Structures of the Welfare State?

Social hackerism is an interesting Finnish example of citizen-created social uses of information technology. It is also an interesting example because it poses important questions about the Finnish informational welfare state. Based on the above analysis of Finnish information-society strategies and their implementation, there are sufficient reasons to conclude that Finland is developing social uses for information technology. In fact, the Finnish information-society project databases list literally hundreds of examples of the social uses of information technology and many of these are very innovative, such as the Macro Pilot.[37] There is a very strong awareness of information technology as a social matter in Finland and, in the long run, this early process, which has involved hundreds of top experts – from the government, companies, universities, and citizens – is likely to have outcomes that are similar to those that sprung from the strong consciousness about technology policy.

But important reservations must be added to this. The Finnish government's inability to advance the Net literacy goal is an example of the significant slowness and the lack of a systematic approach in the implementation of some of its plans. A dynamic government would even provide a platform for citizen initiatives – social hackerism – so that their innovations could spread more systematically. An evaluation study of the well-being cluster project has similar implications. The study notes that because of the project's non dynamic management structure it has not been as open as it could be to companies and research; for example, when thirty private companies formed a spontaneous consortium to work together with the public sector, the project's management rejected the offer.[38]

The concept of the informational welfare state also includes the idea of renewing welfare-state structures through a more dynamic networking organization. Here we see a contradiction between the informational-age goals and the industrial-age structures of the welfare

[37] There are two main databases for the projects: ESIS (European Survey of Information Society: www.ispo.cec.be/esis), compiled by the Information Society Project Office of the EU, and LOCREGIS (LOCal and REGional Information Society: www.kuntaliitto.fi/locregis), compiled by the Finnish Association of Local and Regional Authorities for the EU's main department XVI. At the end of 1997, ESIS listed about 450 Finnish information society projects and LOCREGIS listed about 200 projects. According to Lilius (1998), the biggest financers of these projects were Tekes, the Ministry of Education, the EU, and the municipalities. According to Lilius (1999), there were 142 projects related directly to the second strategy's spearheaded fields.

[38] Pentikäinen (2000). See also Ohinmaa *et al.* (1999).

state. This forms a major challenge that we will discuss in Chapter 8. Of course, it is much easier to face this challenge when the starting-point is the otherwise advanced Finnish informational welfare state, which already combines a dynamic economy with more social justice and collective protection of labor than the global trend and is consciously developing social uses for information technology.

# Chapter 5

# THE LOCAL INFORMATION SOCIETY

## Spatial Dynamics, Information Technology, and Public Policy

*The Spatial Dimension of the Information Society: Metropolitan Nodes and Global Networks*

Space is a fundamental dimension of social structure. Thus, the multi-dimensional transformation from the industrial to the information society includes the emergence of new spatial forms and processes. There has been considerable research on this matter from a compara-tive perspective.[1] It is useful to summarize the main conclusions of this

---

[1] Castells (1999); Mitchell (1999); Wheeler *et al.* (2000); Graham and Marvin (2001).

research, in order to place the spatial dynamics of Finland in a broader context.

In sharp contrast to the predictions of futurologists, instead of the disappearance of cities we are witnessing the largest wave of urbanization in human history. The population of the planet is about to become 50 percent urban, and it is projected to become about two-thirds urban before 2050. Of course, in North America, South America, and Europe, the proportion of urban population, on an average, is already around 80 percent, and growing. In Finland, in 2000, it was 67 percent.[2] Furthermore, the new pattern of urbanization is characterized by the formation of very large urban conurbations, which functionally link previously separated urban centers along transportation axes.

These large metropolitan regions concentrate most of the innovation, directional activities, cultural amenities, and wealth creation capacity in each country and in the world at large. The major metropolitan regions link with each other by telecommunications, the Internet, and fast transportation systems, creating a global architecture of nodes and networks. These innovation and directional functions, globally connected and located in major cities and metropolitan areas are the engines of economic growth and creativity for their hinterlands: local existence depends on the dynamic connection to global networks.

Indeed, the study by Castells and Hall[3] on the major technological centers of the world showed how the information economy is organized, in all countries, around territorially concentrated nodes of innovation, advanced business services, and high-technology manufacturing. Because these metropolitan nodes offer more and better jobs, educational chances, and urban amenities, which attract the most innovative workforce, they are the hubs of the information society, and they are likely to increase their dominance in the foreseeable future

Within these metropolitan regions, there is, in general terms, a spatial process of a concentrated decentralization of population and activities. That is, on the one hand, there is a sprawl of settlements over a vast expanse of territory. But, on the other hand, this sprawl

[2] UNDP (2001).    [3] Castells and Hall (1994).

does not usually take the old form of a separation between the central cities and their suburbs. Instead, there are several centers that structure the sprawl in a multinodal pattern within the metropolitan region. Some of these nodes are formed by new nuclei growing within the pattern of sprawl. But, in most cases, and particularly in Europe, the nodes emerge from the pre-existing urban centers that become articulated with others (of similar or lesser size) by transportation links, and by the spatial interconnection of their production activities, service facilities, and residential areas.

These metropolitan areas concentrate the production of knowledge and the processing of information around a milieux of innovation, and clusters of advanced manufacturing and business services. Thanks to telecommunications and the Internet, these areas can reach out to the entire country and link up with the whole world, while maintaining the concentrated cluster of high value-added activities, thus benefiting from the synergy that is provided by spatial proximity. For instance, Matthew Zook has shown that Internet content providers, measured by the location of Internet domain addresses, are highly concentrated by country and by regions within countries, and are particularly concentrated in certain metropolitan areas, in certain cities, and in certain neighborhoods of these cities.[4] The more an economy becomes informational, the more the population and activities are inclined to concentrate in a few major metropolitan areas, which tend to absorb pre-existing urban centers as nuclei of a new, large area formed by dispersed settlements located along transportation lines. Depending on history, the level of development, and land-use patterns, some of these areas are of high density, others are characterized by low density, some follow freeways, others fast railways, but all tend to follow a similar spatial logic. Namely: concentration of population and activities in major metropolitan nodes that are connected globally and decentralized internally in a multi-nuclear structure of an articulated territorial sprawl. In general terms, and in a worldwide perspective, the Information Age is not the end of the city but the beginning of the megacity. Let us examine how Finland relates to this pattern.

---

[4] Zook (2000, 2001).

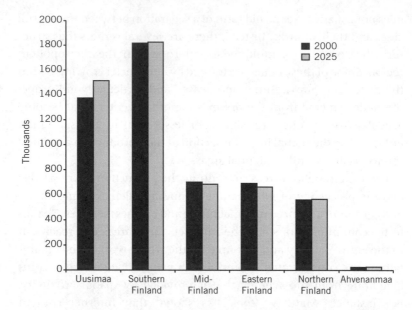

**Fig. 5.1 Population projection by major regions of Finland, 2000–25**

*Source*: Statistics Finland (2000).

## The Metropolitanization of Informational Finland

We cannot pretend, in the framework of this study, to analyze the whole complexity of the territorial transformation of Finland. Our focus is specifically on the relationship between the Finnish information society and spatial dynamics. Figure 5.1 and Map 5.1 show the current general spatial distribution of the population of Finland and its projection to 2025.

In the year 2000, the Uusimaa region around Helsinki accounted for 26.6 percent of the population of the country. On adding the Southern Finland region, comprising Tampere, Turku, and a number of medium-sized cities in the area, the two regions accounted for 61.7 percent of the population. Projections for 2025 show a small increase in the share of both regions: Uusimaa would account for 28.6 percent of the population, and the combined Greater Southern Finland region (Uusimaa plus Southern Finland) would represent 63 percent of the population. In contrast, Northern Finland accounts

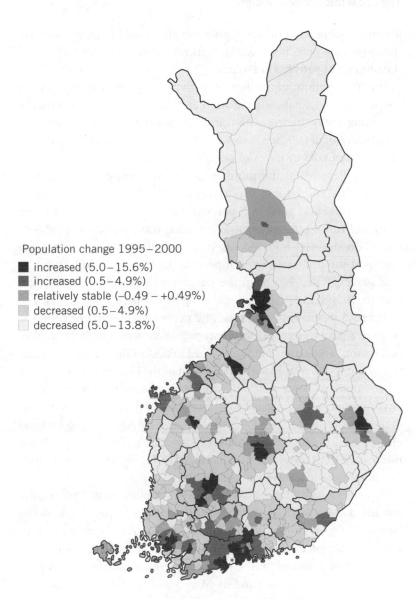

Population change 1995–2000

■ increased (5.0–15.6%)
■ increased (0.5–4.9%)
■ relatively stable (−0.49 – +0.49%)
■ decreased (0.5–4.9%)
☐ decreased (5.0–13.8%)

Map 5.1 The change in population concentration in Finland,
1995–2000

for only 10.9 percent of the population and would remain relatively stable (at 10.8 percent in 2025). This is in historical continuity with the settlement patterns in Finland.

The distribution of economic activity and income generation also follow the spatial concentration around Helsinki, and around the two other major metropolitan areas in Southern Finland, Tampere and Turku (for details, see Map 5.6). Oulu, Lahti, and Jyväskylä are the only counterparts in terms of population concentration, but are of a much smaller size. Furthermore, Helsinki has increased its dominance compared to Tampere and Turku over time. In 1980–5, the population of Greater Helsinki grew by 7 percent, way behind Tampere (13 percent) and Turku (26.8 percent). This trend was reversed in 1985–90, when Greater Helsinki increased its population by a staggering 22.1 percent (followed by Tampere at 19.8 percent and Turku at 13.8 percent). In 1990–5, in the context of a deceleration of urban growth, Helsinki kept its lead, growing by 6.8 percent in contrast to Tampere (5.9 percent) and Turku (4.2 percent). Thus, in principle, we observe a pattern of regional metropolitan concentration of wealth, population, and activity emerging in Finland in line with the world trend. But is this related to the transition to the information society?

We cannot really provide a rigorous answer to this question, but we have attempted an empirical approximation of the issue: the mapping of the Internet domains in Finland. Matthew Zook has researched and elaborated for our study, maps of the spatial distribution of the Internet content providers in Finland. Map 5.2 shows the total number of Internet domains by municipality.

The dominance of Helsinki is clearly demonstrated. Indeed, the conurbation Helsinki/Espoo/Vantaa accounts for 56 percent of all the Finnish Internet domains. The major metropolitan centers follow, with the addition of some key technological centers that are emerging as a result of a deliberate regional development policy. This is confirmed by the data presented in Map 5.3 in which the number of domains is standardized by the population.

Helsinki maintains its leading role as an Internet hub, but it is also joined in the top category by Oulu and Lappeenranta, both sites of universities with strong technology programs. Thus, in line with the findings from the rest of the world, Internet content production is

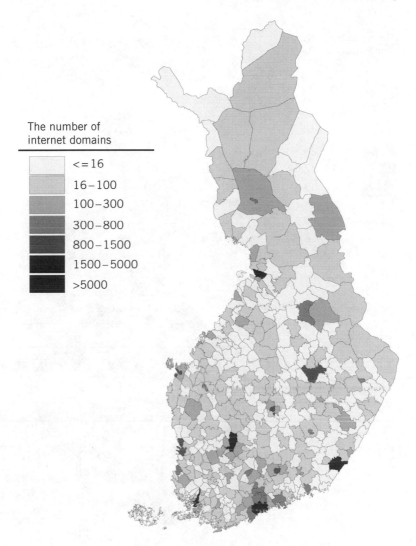

**The number of internet domains**

| | |
|---|---|
| | <=16 |
| | 16-100 |
| | 100-300 |
| | 300-800 |
| | 800-1500 |
| | 1500-5000 |
| | >5000 |

**Map 5.2  The Internet content providers by municipality, 2001**

spatially concentrated around the major metropolitan nodes, the main producers and the consumers of information.

We have also analyzed the spatial concentration of the IT industry in Finland in the context of the European economic geography. For

The number of internet
domains per capita

- 0–0.93
- 0.93–3.17
- 3.17–5.96
- 5.96–9.55
- 9.55–16.14
- 16.14–27.04
- 27.04–55.61

**Map 5.3  The Internet content providers per 1000 population, 2001**

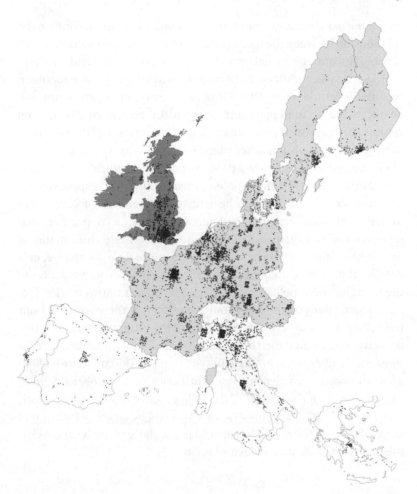

**Map 5.4 The locations of IT related business establishments within the EU**

*Source*: Koski et al. (2001).

this we have relied on the study by Koski, Rouvinen, and Ylä-Anttila, some of whose findings are displayed in Map 5.4.[5]

The map shows that IT production is clearly clustered in a few key metropolitan areas in Europe, one of them being Helsinki. Overall, the spatial concentration of the Internet and of the IT industry in Helsinki,

[5] Koski *et al.* (2001).

and in the main metropolitan centers in Finland, seems to confirm the relationship between the metropolitan information production, the IT capabilities, and the spatial concentration of population and wealth.

However, when we look at the internal structure of the metropolitan regions, it would seem that Finland's metropolitan areas are still characterized by the opposition between the central city, peripheral centers (such as Espoo and Vantaa *vis-à-vis* Helsinki), and the suburbs.[6] Metropolitan expansion takes place from the core to the periphery, along transportation lines, in a process of radioconcentric decentralization. Furthermore, the metropolitan areas of Helsinki/ Espoo/Vantaa, Tampere, and Turku seem to be largely independent of each other in terms of their activities and labor markets. It is possible that if Helsinki/Espoo/Vantaa continue to concentrate informational dynamism, and if Tampere and Turku are not able to engage in a process of info-development, they will ultimately become satellites of the Uusimaa metropolitan region, if and when fast transportation systems (particularly high-speed trains) are built – the current 2-hour transportation time between Helsinki and the other two major metropolitan centers would then be halved. But this is not the situation at the moment. It all depends on the ability of these secondary metropolitan areas to become smaller but relevant nodes of the global network, rather than secondary nodes of the mega-metropolitan region constituted around Helsinki/Espoo/Vantaa. This will be largely a function of the initiatives of the public sector, and particularly of the local governments to dynamize their cities and regions.

## The Challenges of Finnish Spatial Dynamics and the Varying Local Information-Society Responses

The spatial dynamics of Finland raise four major challenges. The first is the depopulation of some peripheral regions. An interesting illustration is offered by Map 5.5, reflecting the aging of the resident population, as an indicator of the threat of depopulation.

---

[6] Anttiroiko (1999*a,b*).

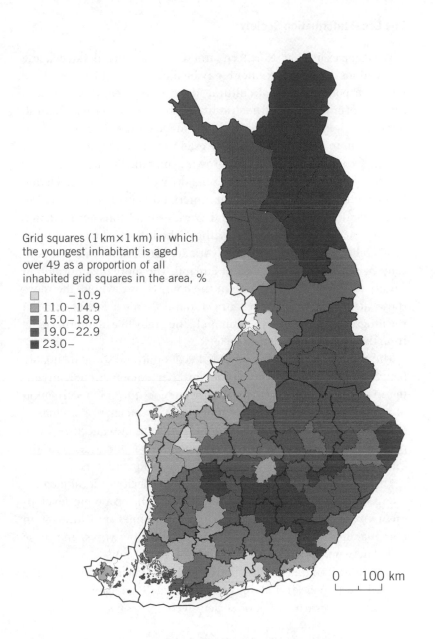

Grid squares (1 km×1 km) in which
the youngest inhabitant is aged
over 49 as a proportion of all
inhabited grid squares in the area, %

- −10.9
- 11.0−14.9
- 15.0−18.9
- 19.0−22.9
- 23.0−

0    100 km

**Map 5.5  The threat of depopulation by the subregional unit**

*Source*: Statistics Finland. Population Statistics 1999. © Statistics Finland 2001.

## The Local Information Society

It is apparent that Northern and Eastern Finland have aging populations whose replacement may be difficult, in which case there will be a potential loss of cultural identity, regional diversity, and a danger of environmental deterioration (this seems to be paradoxical, but we must keep in mind that a man-made nature requires human settlements to maintain the balance established over time).

The second challenge is the growing marginality of rural areas and less-developed regions. As the majority of Finnish people, living in the metropolitan areas and their hinterlands, enter the information society and organize their life and work around Internet-mediated interaction, those communities without the infrastructure and technical ability to connect to the network are functionally and symbolically switched off from the rest of Finland. The more the information society is the mobilizing theme of the country as a whole, the more those lacking the capacity to connect to this theme feel left behind in the progress of the country – ultimately they may live in internal exile from the Finnish information society.

The third challenge is the potential economic and social inequality between Helsinki/Espoo/Vantaa and the other major metropolitan centers. If this gap increases, there will be a tendency toward the formation of a mega-region, with Tampere and Turku as satellites of a dynamic Helsinki area. In this case, there would be an extreme concentration of population, congestion of Helsinki/Espoo/Vantaa, and a decay of the infrastructure and services of the other metropolitan centers.

The fourth challenge is the diminishing capacity of local governments, outside the Helsinki area, to cope with the economic development of their localities, as their local economies and innovation potential depend on their connection to global networks, and these global networks privilege their connection to Helsinki.

Institutional and grassroot responses to these challenges constitute the set of projects, policies, and outcomes aimed at building what we characterize as the local information society. It comprises five dimensions:

- National policies of IT-led regional development.
- Local initiatives of cooperative regional development, supported by national and European institutions.

- Grassroot efforts to build citizen participation.
- Grassroot efforts, supported by public policies, to integrate rural areas and less-developed regions into the information society.
- Local policies of comprehensive informational development.

We will analyze these various aspects of the local information society by focusing on specific examples of projects that illustrate the issues under consideration without exhausting the subject.

## Regional Development in the Information Society: The View from the Top

Regional development has been a concern of the Finnish national governments for decades. The need to prevent depopulation of the less-developed areas of the country is part of the preservation of national identity. Since the 1960s, Finnish strategies of national development focused on the uses of higher education, research, and technology as engines of regional economic growth.

A major policy initiative in this sense was the decision, implemented from the 1960s onwards, to create new universities all around the country, with a particular emphasis on engineering and technology. Before then, only Helsinki and Turku had full universities. In the following two decades, the number of Finnish universities increased to twenty, and these new universities, in particular the technology-oriented universities, appear to have played a major role in stimulating the regional growth in peripheral regions and cities in an industrial transition. Key examples are Tampere, where the two new universities are among the leading Finnish universities and play an important role in the transformation of Tampere into an important informational development center; Oulu, nowadays an IT-led growth pole that has become the fourth major metropolitan node in Finland, anchoring population in the Northern/Central Finland region; and Lappeenranta, one of the few prosperous towns in Eastern Finland.

## The Local Information Society

It would seem, as a general trend, that the policy of creating universities and decentralizing them has been a major factor in stimulating the regional economic development around new growth centers supported by knowledge and information-processing capacity in these university towns. As an illustration, we have plotted in Map 5.6 the levels of GDP per capita and the location of technical universities, as well as universities that include a technical component.

The parallelism is striking. A rigorous analysis would require a multiple regression model, including a number of control variables, but we suggest the hypothesis of a direct and positive relationship between the location of technical universities and the dynamics of local/regional economic growth.

The other major technology-based policy related to local/regional development was, as in many other countries of the world, the creation of technology parks, subsidized by the national agencies and the local governments. As is the case in other countries, the record of these technology parks as sources of regional development is mixed.[7] On the one hand, when these projects were connected to a strong technical university, and were embedded into a broader network of industrial companies, as was the case in Oulu, they contributed to the expansion of the technological foundation of new industrial clusters. However, left to themselves, technology parks generated little synergy. For example, Vuorinen *et al.* showed that many companies located in the parks seemed to have stronger ties with firms outside the park than with their neighbors.[8] Spatial proximity, and even the presence of universities in the vicinity, cannot act as a substitute for a network of cooperation developed from the inner dynamics of the industry. In other words, technology parks are stimulants of economic growth only when and where they are connected to a broader cluster of innovation.

Over time, national technology policy has evolved toward supporting the private and public actors in regional development (firms, local governments, community initiatives) in their entrepreneurial initiatives, rather than initiating programs on the basis of national priorities. It appears to be a more fruitful strategy.

---

[7] Castells and Hall (1994).      [8] Vuorinen *et al.* (1989).

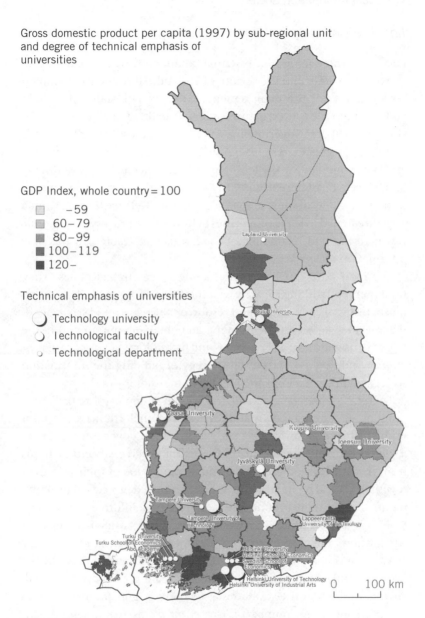

Gross domestic product per capita (1997) by sub-regional unit and degree of technical emphasis of universities

GDP Index, whole country = 100

- -59
- 60-79
- 80-99
- 100-119
- 120-

Technical emphasis of universities

- Technology university
- Technological faculty
- Technological department

Lapland University

Oulu University

Vaasa University

Kuopio University

Joensuu University

Jyväskylä University

Tampere University

Tampere University of Technology

Lappeenranta University of Technology

Turku University
Turku School of Economics
Åbo Akademy

Helsinki University
Helsinki School of Economics
Swedish School of Economics

Helsinki University of Technology
Helsinki University of Industrial Arts

0          100 km

**Map 5.6  The GDP per capita and the location of universities with strong technology programs**

*Source*:  Statistics Finland. Regional account 1997. © Statistics Finland 2001.

117

## Local Networking for Regional Development

Local governments are an essential component of the relationship between the state and the society in Finland. They assume the main responsibility for the management of the welfare state, they build and maintain the infrastructure, and are the first line of contact with citizens. The Local Government Act of 1995 increased their functions, and granted greater responsibility. On the other hand, tax income and state subsidies for the local governments decreased substantially in the recession of the early 1990s. Furthermore, the growing concentration of an economic dynamism in the Helsinki/Espoo/Vantaa area threatened to leave other cities behind in the process of economic restructuring and technological modernization leading to the new information society.

The local governments reacted along three strategic lines. They used their networking capacity around the regional councils to set up mechanisms of cooperation and resource sharing, around strategies of regional development. They sought, and obtained, the support of the EU, with its wide range of regional- and technology-development programs. And they embraced the strategy of building the information society, giving to it a local and regional dimension.

There are nineteen regional councils in Finland (plus the autonomous government of Åland). These regional councils are joint municipal boards, formed on the basis of local governments. These regional councils are the institutions that receive structural funds from the EU. Using these funds, and putting some of their resources together, several regional councils have launched projects of development, usually built around the notion of the information society. One of the most ambitious was the Project for Applying Regional Applications for Developing a Democratic Information Society (PARADDIS). Supported by the EU, it was undertaken in 1998 by the West Finland Alliance, including the five regions of Central Finland, Ostrobothnia, South Ostrobothnia, Satakunta, and Tampere. It was aimed at supporting a number of IT-based programs to stimulate job generation and economic competitiveness in the region. These projects included telematic services for the small and medium businesses; the development of content for the multimedia industry; distance learning; telework; telemedicine; and democratic participation on-line. Five projects were selected: the open Net service; the municipal service information system; the information society concept for municipalities; the development of production methods and processes for new media; and electronic commerce. It is still too early to evaluate them, but they are all based on cooperation between municipal services, local firms, and local users.

Other development projects are built on *ad hoc* regional networks on the basis of voluntary inter-municipal cooperation, although some of them are coordinated by private companies (e.g., Digital City Oulu), research institutes (Networking Project in Ylä-Savo), or technical universities (e.g., the Information Network of Satakunta). Among examples of these regional network projects we can cite: the Free Access to Regional Intranet and Internet services of the Hämeenlinna region, offering low-cost access to the Internet for citizens and small businesses; the Suupohja Information Network Project, to provide access and training for small businesses, municipalities, schools, and colleges in the area; the Information Network of Koillismaa, to serve the communication needs of the resident population of a sparsely inhabited area; the Regional Electronic Network of the Ii Region, to promote networking and the exchange of information between public institutions and social and economic actors in the region, including the transfer of innovation from the regional technopolis centers to the rest of the region. Most of these programs deliver information and facilitate access to information systems in the hope that information and networking will result in an enhanced local capability for informational development. It still has to be assessed whether the link between information and regional development is straightforward, or if it requires a more complex developmental loop.

Overall, reflecting on the practice of these projects, two of the leading researchers in this field, Anttiroiko and Savolainen, summarize their findings as follows: "The Internet is used by local authorities mainly for conventional marketing, not for teledemocratic experiments or empowerment. The utilization of ICTs and new applications have not so far brought with them any deep changes in the organizational and democratic processes."[9] According to these researchers, networking is changing the structures of governance at the local and regional level. Telematic services are improving, but there is a very limited range of transactions and interactive services. Knowledge management is improving in the local governments. However, overall "the whole idea of the Information Society [in the projects of local governments] looks very techno-centered."

In our own assessment, many of these projects do not go very far beyond improving Internet access, and facilitating Internet networking faster and more equitably than commercial services. They have also contributed to the technological modernization of the local governments and stimulated their networking. However, their contribution to economic growth is rather limited unless they are integrated into a broader development strategy, as in the case of Tampere, which we examine below. Their contribution to local democracy and citizen participation is, for the time being, merely symbolic.

## Local Teledemocracy?

There are, however, some isolated experiments in socio-political innovation, such as Espoo's Idea Factory. Electronic public services are an explicit goal of the second information-society strategy of the Finnish government. Government action has thus focused on developing ways of giving information on the Net and on creating an electronic identity system to make this possible. The main projects have been the Ministry of the Interior's electronic public services project called JUNA, the Ministry of Finance's public services portal project, and an electronic ID card that would provide the technological "infrastructure" for advanced electronic commerce and public services.

But these are still mainly just plans. However, Idea Factory – another example of social hackerism – is in actual use.[10] It is a Net-based facility for the young people of Espoo, the second biggest city in Finland

---

[9] Anttiroiko and Savolainen (1999: 425).
[10] Cf. www.nettiparlamentti.fi/ideafactory. This information is also based on discussions with the project's leader, Ari Tammi.

(in practice part of the larger Helsinki area), to present their ideas to local decision-makers. The process begins when someone presents an idea on the Net. Then the other young people criticize it and develop it further. Ultimately, a motion is formed and a vote follows. If the motion passes, the young can collect signatures for it. The Espoo youth council then presents the initiative to the city council and/or gets media attention for the idea. The Idea Factory moderators monitor how the idea is progressing in the council.

The users of the Idea Factory have been between 13 and 20 years old. They have formulated local initiatives based on the needs that they have, which are not represented by the adult members of the city council, such as skate parks and setting aside unused space for the use of the young. The Idea Factory platform has also been used more generally; for example, for the planning of a new tram line in Helsinki.

While this is a limited experiment, it shows the potentially fruitful uses of the Internet to foster democratic participation, particularly among the most politically alienated sector of society: young people, who are heavy users of the Internet but only occasional participants in local democracy – indeed, minors are completely disfranchised. In this sense, Espoo may be breaking new ground for future forms of democratic participation.

## Sustaining Regional Community in the Information Society: The Upper Karelia Learning Project

Upper Karelia provides an example of another local information-society strategy: sustaining the regional community and integrating it into the information society.[11] Upper Karelia is a poor rural area in the eastern forest periphery of Finland with a population of about 20 000. As a consequence of the declining incomes in agriculture and forestry, it has a high level of unemployment and out-migration of young people.

---

[11] The following analysis is mainly based on our visit to North Karelia in December 2000. Additional information has been obtained from Oksa and Turunen (2000a,b) and Saarelainen (2000).

## The Local Information Society

The idea for a social information-society project was formed by a group of local people. They were able to obtain support from the Regional Council of North Karelia and from Sitra. The project started in April 1998. Twenty-one local unemployed people were trained to become Net trainers and support persons in six months at the local Nurmes Vocational Training Center. These former unemployed turned Net experts then started to teach Net skills to local people. More than thirty Net kiosks, which provided free public Net access, were established in libraries, youth centers, club houses for unemployed people, local banks, and shops. The Net trainers have taught Net skills to people at these kiosks, in separate courses at schools, at village meetings, in a senior "drive-in" (where people over 60 can drop in to learn about the Net), and in the home (also helping to install the necessary hardware and software). Another seventeen Net trainers were trained from unemployed students at the beginning of the project's second year. All training and support have been free and easily available.

The project's main creation has been a community network where people communicate with each other and local actors share information for free (including a very popular flea-market). Within two years of the project's start, 25 percent of the population had registered as local Net users and created a local Net culture. The local learning model is now being transferred to ten other peripheral regions, funded by Sitra. Ilpo Koskikallio, the key local person behind the project, has set up a company called Glocal that is planning to expand its activity to the other regions of Finland and Europe and thus become a service exporter from North Karelia (know-how about local community building by and around Internet use).

The key to the success of the Upper Karelia learning project has been its high "local intelligence." All key actors were local and thus very sensitive to the real needs and skill levels of local people. The project leader, Koskikallio, with his family, moved many years ago from Helsinki to Nurmes, leaving his job as a teacher to become a farmer. Nowadays, he is a farmer, a teacher of the Internet, a social activist, and an entrepreneur of know-how on the local information society.

But he may be one of the few cases of actual entrepreneurial development directly resulting from the program (another was the group of unemployed turned Net experts who founded a Net-training company).

Also, despite its success in community building and diffusing the use of the Internet, the project was not as good in advancing the Net skills of the adult population as those of the young (whereas almost all people under 20 years used the local network, only about a fifth of the adults between 30 and 60 used it, and use by the seniors was virtually non-existent). Furthermore, the direct economic impact of the program seems to be rather limited. Regional development means, essentially, creating jobs in the region. And the diffusion of Internet use, in itself, does not increase employment. Economic development strategies require the creation of business with the specific capacity to compete. For instance, one of the largest companies in the region, Tulikivi, specializes in producing artistic fireplaces and stoves made of soap stone. They export all over the world, including to Hollywood stars in California, in spite of the heavy weight of their product. Although Tulikivi obviously uses the Internet, and has an advanced production technology, it is not an Internet-based company that can directly use the skills provided by the project. It is, largely, an independent development. Only if a number of similar industrial/agricultural/forestry/tourism entrepreneurial initiatives take root in Upper Karelia will the region be able to avoid depopulation.

However, the Upper Karelia learning project, while not constituting a strategy of regional development, has important positive effects for the region. First, it diffuses the basic Internet literacy that helps people, particularly the young, to improve their educational opportunities, and may even help them in their search for jobs, should economic development prospects materialize. Second, it builds and strengthens the community, as we were able to observe, so that local societies endure in their vitality, in their local ties, in their traditions, and experience their joint strength by engaging in new projects. Third, and most important, at a time when Finland is fully committed to building an information society by and around the Internet, people in Upper Karelia feel that they are also a part of it. They are not marginalized by the new technological paradigm, they know what the Internet is, and they are connected to the global networks from their local existence. Glocal is indeed a fitting name for this innovative project that has succeeded in sustaining identity and meaning in a spatially rooted experience, while connecting to the global networks of the information society.

## The Making of a Local Information Society as a Development Strategy: eTampere

Tampere serves as an example of our fifth type of Finnish local informa-tion-society response: informational development.[12] In the 1980s and 1990s, Tampere underwent an arduous and ultimately successful transition from an old manufacturing town to a high-technology cluster. This cluster includes major telecommunication and multi-media companies like Nokia, Sonera, Alma-Media, Tampere Telephone Cooperative, Tellia, Tellabs, and the National Broadcasting Company (TV2), which form the core of a diversified high-technology sector that employed around 15 000 workers in 2000. A key resource for this eco-nomic restructuring was the quality of the universities, Tampere University of Technology and the University of Tampere, and the strong emphasis of these universities on information technology, and linking up with industrial firms to advance research and development in cutting-edge communication technologies and their applications.

In 1995, the city of Tampere created a Tampere Region Center of Expertise Program, with an emphasis on mechanical engineering and automation, information and communication technology, media services, knowledge-intensive business services, and health-care technology. This program was built around three main technological nodes: the first was the Health Care Technology Center Finn-Medi, and the development company Finn-Medi Research, co-owned by the city of Tampere, the University of Tampere, Sitra, Finnvera, and other partners. The second node was the Technology Center Hermia, a partnership between the city and the Tampere University of Technology, and the third was the Finlayson Media Center, supporting the develop-ment of new media and IT companies, and symbolically located in the building of an old garment factory.

On the basis of this experience, in 2000, the city of Tampere and the Tampere urban region, in cooperation with the universities and several firms, launched a new project, eTampere, within the frame-work of the eEurope programme created in 1999 by the European

---

[12] Cf. *www.etampere.fi*. We have also received additional information from Juha Kostiainen, Business Development Director, city of Tampere.

Commissioner for the Information Society, Erkki Liikanen. The project aims at positioning Tampere as "a key city within the global Information Society by strengthening its knowledge base, generating new business, and creating new public online services." The originality of the program is that it aims to develop a local information society, around the expansion of public services, that would constitute a local market and an experimentation ground for new information and communication goods and services, whose development would allow the creation and expansion of new businesses. A series of technology programs in key areas of social interaction would provide the infrastructure for innovation. The connection between social uses and marketable products would be facilitated by the new University of Tampere's Information Society Institute, in which social researchers would explore social trends, needs, and behavior to ensure a citizen-driven, consumer-driven, social uses-driven expansion of information technologies. Indeed, the strategic vision put forward by the city of Tampere is that "the next phase [of the information society] is the scientific convergence of information technology/media and social sciences (psychology, sociology, economics etc.) which will produce a new paradigm where new technology and new media will slowly join in a new interpretation. The same will take place at a practical level, that is a real Information Society will emerge where technologies and media that are perceived as new at the moment become an organic part of society and of the everyday life of people and technology will lose its value as such."

Accordingly, the eTampere program brings together in a coordinated effort several programs and institutions:

- Five "engine technologies" lines of research and development, developed by the Digital Media Institute of Tampere University of Technology, which focus on adaptive software components, user interfaces, perception of information, neoreality (a fancy new name for what used to be called 3D virtual reality), and broadband data transfer.
- A research and evaluation laboratory, set up by the VTT Technical Research Center of Finland, to test and evaluate new products in their final stages of development.

- An eTampere "business accelerator," another catchy term for an innovative combination of a business incubator and monitored venture capital investment, which aims to enable five businesses every year to be listed in public offerings on the stock market.
- An eBusiness Research Center at the Tampere University of Technology to provide the necessary knowledge and training in management.
- The above-mentioned Information Society Institute at the University of Tampere, which focuses on the social knowledge of information technology and its interaction with society.
- And Infocity, a program of the city of Tampere, with a broad range of services and interactive information for its citizens, thus creating a vast field of experimentation for online services, at home, school, work, and on the move.

It is obviously too early to evaluate a program that only started in 2001. The program's self-presentation is often couched in the naïve terms of futurology.

Yet, the fundamental concept behind these words appears to be a major innovation on the prior policies of high-technology development. Indeed, the current trends in the expansion of the information society, worldwide, point toward the increasing importance of the social uses of information technology. Beyond business use, the consumption of Internet services and information technology devices is increasingly driven by new uses decided by the public and society. To investigate how society adopts and shapes new information technologies, to advance research and development programs along these lines, and to support and launch new businesses on the basis of these strategic anticipations, is a bold project that could bring prosperity to Tampere and innovation to the world at large. However, as with so many other projects, the actual outcome will depend on the implementation, and on the ability of the managers of the program to follow people's needs and uses instead of their technological logic and personal vision of society. If eTampere lives up to its expectations, it should be remembered that it was a local initiative that was supported by the EU as an example of the local state and the European network state, building networks of cooperation in order to innovate in business and society.

Chapter 6

# THE POWER OF IDENTITY
## Identity Driving the Information Society and the Information Society Building Identity

It is important to remember that the theory of the network society is not just an analysis of the rise of the global informational economy. The core of the theory is the tension between the rise of the network society and cultural identity.[1] The dominant global trend is that the progress of the global informational economy creates a strong resistance, based on the experience that the development threatens

---

[1] Castells (2000*a*).

cultural identities. Thus, nationalism and religious fundamentalism are increasing with the rise of the network society. The contradiction between the Net and the self is the contradiction between the global information society and the values of the people. For example, many people fear that the global information society means Western values worldwide. The big question is how the information society can relate to different cultural identities and form a positive interaction between the self and the Net, instead of conflict. Or, to phrase the question differently, the big challenge is: can there be a legitimizing relationship between identity and the information society?

## The Finnish Information Society and Identity

One factor that makes Finland interesting, in the global context, is its lack of strong resistance identities. There is no ultra-nationalist movement, as there is in many other European countries, including other Nordic countries (e.g. the popularity of the People's Party in Denmark and the Progress Party in Norway). There is no significant religious fundamentalism, as there is even in the United States. As we saw, the crime level is low. And, there is no strong anti-globalization movement.

Why is this? Our analysis is that it is the result of a relationship between the information society and identity that is different from the global trend. The Finnish model of the information society is built on the Finnish identity. The integration of the information society in Finland with the welfare state – which mitigates the socially divisive impact of the information society and makes the success of the information society a financial basis of the welfare state – has been a major reason for the lack of a strong resistance against the information society in Finland. In fact, we can go even further: the source of legitimacy is not only the integrated model; the two components of the Finnish model – the information society and the welfare state – are also separately rooted deep in the Finnish identity. Let us give this notion more substance.[2]

---

[2] Of course, a comprehensive analysis of Finnish identity would merit a book of its own and we do not pretend to attempt such a daunting enterprise here. We focus only on the most relevant factors for the Finnish information society and the welfare state. For more general approaches on the Finnish identity, see Klinge (1991, 1993); Korhonen (1993); Apo and Ehrnrooth (1996); Laaksonen and Mettomäki (1996); Hannula (1997); Alasuutari and Ruuska (1998); Löytönen and Kolbe (1999).

## A History of Survival

The first matter to consider in understanding both these elements of Finnish identity is Finland's history of survival. By survival, we mean here biological-economic and political-cultural survival. Finland is Europe's northern frontier. For most of Finland's history, the cold winters have been, literally, a challenge to survival. The summers were a preparation for the winter and if the winter lasted longer than the average or the summer was not warm enough, the lost harvest made the following winter even harder. The cold has killed more Finns than war. And this is not too far back in history.

Finland has existed as an independent country for only three generations, and many grandparents of the present third generation have themselves experienced hunger and eaten *pettuleipa*, an emergency bread made from pine bark.[3] The most extreme example is as recent as the so-called Hunger Years of 1867–8 when cold weather first delayed the sowing of the crop and then an unusually early frost at the beginning of September destroyed the harvest. The result of these catastrophic years was the death of an estimated 120 000 Finns or 6.5 percent of the population.

Economically, Finland has been a poor country for most of its history. It was an agrarian or even subsistence economy much longer than other European countries, with most Finns living as peasants. As late as the beginning of the 1950s, Finland could be considered fundamentally an agrarian society, with about half of the population still in agriculture (70 percent at the beginning of the twentieth century). The 1950s marked Finland's change into an industrial society and then, during the last quarter of the twentieth century, Finland developed into a wealthy information society. But, as late as the beginning of the 1990s, Finland went through an exceptionally deep recession, which was again experienced as a battle of survival.

The second dimension of the Finnish history of survival is in its political-cultural context. Finland is located between the West and the East. The survival of the Finnish nation has never been guaranteed. From the thirteenth century until the beginning of the nineteenth

[3] See Häkkinen (1992).

century, Finland was a part of Sweden. Then, for more than a century, Finland was a part of Russia. However, even after its formal independence in 1917, Finland has had to do its best to prevent itself from becoming a part of the Soviet Union or Germany.[4] World War II was a critical time for Finland: first the Soviet Union attacked it in November 1939 (the Winter War), and then Finland was compelled to enter into a war alliance with Germany and allow the latter to use its land for an attack on the Soviet Union in 1941, bringing German soldiers to Finland and threatening the future of its independence.

Since World War II, Finnish national survival has depended on a balancing act between the West and the Soviet Union. The Soviet Union forced Finland to sign a YYA Treaty (Treaty of Friendship, Cooperation, and Mutual Assistance) in 1948, as it had done with other Eastern European countries (although the terms of the Finnish treaty were significantly different whereby it was not a Soviet satellite). At times, the Soviet Union has tried to dictate Finland's politics very directly and the pressure on Finland's independence was considerable. Only since the collapse of the Soviet Union in 1991 has Finland been totally free of Soviet influence, although Finns continue to remember that Russia is their neighbor and that its powerlessness is only temporary. Finally, since Finland applied for membership in the EU just a couple of months after the collapse of the Soviet Union and became a full member at the beginning of 1995, there is the new question of surviving as a sovereign nation in the European network state (although this is an issue that Finland shares with all other members of the EU).

Related to the political survival of the nation, the survival of national culture has been an important question, particularly the fate of the Finnish language. Under the control of Sweden and then Russia, Finnish was not the language of the ruling class in the country. Until the end of the nineteenth century, most cultural expressions were in Swedish. As a consequence, the preservation and creation of the Finnish culture

[4] For the development of Finland's independence, see e.g. Jussila (1987); Singleton (1989); Alapuro (1994). Here it is important to add that it would be anachronistic to interpret the Finnish project so that there was always a strongly unified nation of Finns who wanted to found their own state. The understanding that Finns have of themselves has changed throughout history – the nineteenth-century ideology of the nation-state was especially important in the formation of the present idea of the Finnish nation.

became very much related to the project of asserting Finland as a nation. For example, Finnish media and literature developed very much as a nationalist project guided by the principle of "one language, one nation." The national epos, *Kalevala*, was published in the mid-nineteenth century based on a long oral tradition but deliberately edited to construct a mythical Finnish history. Characteristically, the old authors that have been elevated to the status of national heroes have written about World War II (Väinö Linna's *Unknown Soldier*) or the language itself (Aleksis Kivi's *Seven Brothers*, a story of seven Finns learning to read Finnish).

## The Information Society as a New Survival Project and a Legitimizer of the Nation-State

Together, the Finnish biological-economic and political-cultural survival struggles have created a quest for a "post-survival" Finland. There are several important identity factors that are derived from this history for the Finnish information society. As a result, in Finnish history, the state receives its legitimacy by asserting national survival. The Finnish state was born as a survival project and each government has to convince the population that its program guarantees the continuation of the Finnish nation. The development of the information society has become a new survival project that legitimizes the state as long as the people can see that it advances Finland's survival.

On the other hand, the strong Finnish national identity – relying on ethnic homogeneity and a common language, without being ultra-nationalist – is an important basis for the development of the information society. Finland has a history of coming together for a national project: today, the Winter War and the reconstruction of Finland after the devastation of World War II have been replaced as a collective project by the building of the information society, which developed into a key theme in the context of surviving the recession of the early 1990s.

## The Orientation toward the Future

Yet, Finnish identity does not just drive the information society; it is also being built on the information society. The short and fragile history of Finland as an independent country is significant in understanding how the information society became, and remains, an identity-building project. In historical terms, Finland is a rather new project: many grandparents of the younger generation lived under Russian rule. The Finns do not feel that their country has come of age, unlike other European countries with thousands of years of history. The information-society project suits a young country that is still partly in search of an identity. With little history to build their identity on, the Finns are oriented to the future. For Finland, the "post-survival" culture is something that is being created now; looking forward and not backward.

But the future is also something to be concerned about. Futurology has had an exceptionally strong presence in Finland since the 1970s. Various research institutes, like Sitra, and ministries have published numerous reports containing possible scenarios for the future of their subject, with titles along the lines of *X in 2017* (where X is Finland, the economy, education, social policy, and so on). Since the beginning of the 1990s, Parliament has even required the government to present the so-called Report on the Future to Parliament, and – the only parliament in the world to do this – it has a separate Committee for the Future.[5]

This orientation toward the future has clearly made the transformation of Finland into an information society easier than in some older European cultures, which carry with them a long cultural history. However, it is important to add that not all of this attitude should be attributed to Finnishness. It is also a structural feature of the informational economy, in which companies and even countries compete in the context of the culture of speed by promising that the future will arrive faster through them than through their competitors. This image-making is important for success in the informational economy, and the image of a futurist country can also be seen as a general sign of an advanced informational economy. There has been more or less the same trait in Japan and in California, for example.

---

[5] The recession, in particular, generated a lot of this kind of future-oriented literature, including e.g. Riihinen (1992); Vartia and Ylä-Anttila (1992); Council of the State (1993); Lehtisalo (1994); Ruokanen and Nurmio (1995).

## A Positive Attitude to Technology

Finnish enthusiasm for technology has been noted by foreign observers since the end of the nineteenth century. For example, Angel Ganivet, the Spanish author and consul to Finland in 1896–7, wrote in his *Cartas Finlandesas* (Finnish Letters) that in Finland "there are almost as many phones as kitchenware."[6] There seems to be a link between the positive Finnish attitude to technology and the country's history of survival. Of course, it is well known that natural conditions like climate do not offer a real explanation of a nation's development. There is, for example, no logic in the idea that, because the Finnish winters are so cold that one cannot do anything else, so one starts developing information technology – otherwise Greenland would be the most advanced information society in the world and nothing would have happened in sunny Silicon Valley (and you can do other things indoors besides programming). However, in more complex ways *and* in interaction with other more important factors, natural conditions do play a part.

Survival has characterized Finnish history and, in fact, it is only for two generations that Finns have not had to live with an eye to the coming winter *thanks to technology*. From a historical viewpoint, a life without the struggle for survival is a new experience in Finland, which technology has made possible. In its struggle to survive, the Finnish attitude has been very pragmatic: if a new tool could help, it has been welcomed without the kind of skepticism about a technological way of life that has been strong in older, and more favorably located, European cultures. Finland has undeniably been an exceptionally technology-positive country, which has been among the first in the world to adopt for use everything from the electric light to the telephone.

One can argue that in Finland technology has been related to the pursuit of a "post-survival" life. Finns do not see technology in contradiction to culture but as a tool for creating a new culture here and now. Some would call this "victory over nature," but in the Finnish context it is not the industrial idea of subordinating nature. Instead,

[6] Ganivet (1905).

Finns continue to relate very closely to nature: the idea of spending the weekend in one's own cottage in the middle of the forest by a lake, warming up a sauna with hand-chopped wood and swimming even in freezing water, still remains a national ideal.

## The Minority Attitude

There is also something distinct in Finnish identity as a result of Finland's history of survival. The experience of being part of another power has shaped Finnish identity as a "minority identity." The Finns were a suppressed minority for almost eight hundred years and became the majority in their country only three generations ago. One cannot expect a nation's historical identity to change completely in so short a time, especially as the Finns continue to experience themselves as a minority in the world (Finland's population of 5.2 million people constitutes less than a thousandth of the planet's population). The strange fact is that, even after becoming the majority in their country, Finns continue to think of themselves as a minority. As will be discussed in more detail in Chapter 8, this is a source of difficulty when relating to the multiculturalism, which is increasing with the global information society.

There has been much discussion of the Finnish national experience of inferiority and it is something that really influences Finnish culture. The feeling of inferiority seems to be best explained as a minority attitude. Because of this feeling of inferiority, the image of Finland as seen by others has been very important for Finns. Even today, recognition from the rest of the world is felt to be particularly significant. Also, against the background of having always been a minority, in second place to someone else, the idea of winning has gained exceptional importance. It should be remembered that, until very recently, the Finns as a national team had never won in any international sports events (not even in ice hockey, the national sport, in which Finland won the world championship for the first time in 1995, the time of Nokia's rise). The idea of becoming the world's "number one" information society must be understood against the background of boosting national self-esteem.

For Finns, the information society is a new identity, which is designed to replace the earlier images of Finland as a forest economy or a satellite of the Soviet Union. Information technology is, for Finland, a way to show to itself and to the world that it is no longer a poor or subdued country. Of course, this way of reacting to the "colonialist" history under Sweden and the Soviet Union is – despite its sometimes amusing tones – more productive than national bitterness because it is about orienting Finland toward what can be done in the future.

## The Welfare State as a Post-Survival State and a Legitimizer of the Nation-State

Together, the above factors have created the Finnish information-society project as something that is not just based on Finnish identity but is also a project of building that identity. The same is largely true of the Finnish welfare state.

### The Ideologies of "Post-Survival" Life

The two ideological roots of the Finnish welfare state are the nineteenth- and twentieth-century social movements (the labor movement and the women's movement) and the Protestant religion.[7] It would be too much to say that they were directly created by survival struggles, but they were certainly intensified by them. The suffering of the workers in the Hunger Years was an important trigger in the formation of the Finnish labor movement. In the nineteenth century, the women's movement was also closely related to charity work in the survival struggles. Since then, Finnish women have been central in building a welfare state based on the ideas of equality and inclusion. In fact, continuing the active political role of Finnish women (which includes the fact that they were the first to acquire the right to vote in Europe in 1906), they took an especially central decision-making role in shaping the Finnish welfare state, beginning in the 1960s.

---

[7] For a more political history of the Finnish welfare state, see Haatanen (1992) and Haatanen and Suonoja (1992).

Many aspects of the Finnish welfare state were actually created to give women the same opportunities as men: women's entry into the job market was made possible by the introduction of a long, paid parental leave, high-quality subsidized children's day care, free school meals, and so on.

The second source of the Finnish welfare state can be found in the Protestant religion, and is based on the Lutheran emphasis on pursuing an equal society rather than individual merit by acts (grace saves, not personal development). The Finnish welfare society is essentially a social interpretation of the principle "Love thy neighbor as thyself." It is the Christian idea of imagining yourself in a different place in society, and thus building a just society from the viewpoint of not knowing in which situation you may find yourself. About 85 percent of Finns continue to belong to the Protestant church,[8] and it continues to influence Finnish identity even more widely.

*The Experience of "We"*

Another important factor behind the Finnish welfare state can be related to the particular history of Finnish survival. That is the Finnish experience of a national "we" that links Finns together. By this notion, we mean, on the one hand, the ability to form networks of direct and informal communication among this "us." This ability can be seen as an adaptation to the conditions in which Finns have had to act. For eight hundred years, the Finns were controlled by a non-Finnish group, which made the Finns part of a relatively homogeneous peasant class.[9] There was a top-down hierarchy between the powers-that-be and the Finns but not much differentiation among the Finns themselves who were, compared to other societies, more on the same horizontal level and had to network with each other to manage. As a consequence, most Finns are from a relatively close social background and treat each other in communication as equals based on origin from the same class (and often knowing each other through some relative or friendship link).

The experience of a "we" also means the idea of leaving no one behind, which was strengthened by the Finnish survival battles, especially

---

[8] Statistics Finland (2000).
[9] For a detailed history of the Finnish peasantry, see e.g. Jutikkala (1958).

during World War II. The Soviet Union's attack on Finland in November 1939 started the famous Winter War, in which the Finns stood united against the much bigger and better armed military force of the Soviet Union. A peace treaty was signed in March 1940. As mentioned above, Finland became involved in World War II again in the so-called Continuation War 1941–4, a war that it lost but in which it managed to confirm its independence. The experience of World War II – and, related to it, the reconstruction of Finland, the paying of the war indemnity to the Soviet Union, and the international recognition of Finland's independence – united the nation socially through struggling together. The war made the Finns think of themselves even more strongly as a cohesive group, which has strong solidarity and does not leave any members behind.

Together these factors have created the identity basis for the Finnish welfare state, whose goal is to guarantee a "post-survival" life for all of "us." This welfare state has given Finland a less money-driven identity, which supports the kind of hackerism that Linux represents, and innovating in the social uses of information technology, as in the case of social hackerism.

## Divided Identity

But Finnish identity has also been divided. In fact, Finnish identity has gone through a process that could easily have taken Finland to a very different outcome. The critical testing moments came just after 1917 when Finland became independent. (Finland used the opportunity of the Russian Revolution to declare itself independent just a month after the end of that revolution.) One might expect that a nation that had finally become independent would be united for its development. However, without a direct external threat to survival, the Finns became divided against each other. A bloody civil war started in January 1918, just one month after independence, between the Reds (socialists) and the Whites (non-socialists) with opposing social interests and very different views of Finland's future. After the two-month war, 35 000 people or 1 percent of the population were dead, 30 000 of the dead were Reds out of which 12 000 died as a result of the prison camps, a dark chapter in Finnish history.[10] Until the 1930s, the conflict between the Red and White ideology continued in different ways; another civil war was avoided but violence continued under different forms. For example, the right-wing Lapua movement used direct violence against socialists and progressives in general.[11] In fact, Finland oscillated between its fragile democracy and its totalitarian tendencies.

The uniting of the nation was under way in the late 1930s but, as was mentioned, it was significantly accelerated by World War II. Other political factors contributed towards the Finnish welfare state and the information society after the war: communism was avoided by channeling socialist thinking into the construction of the welfare state and Western Europe was approached in an ideologically neutral way by joining its technology development.

Of course, it should be remembered that the testing of Finnish identity is by no means limited to history. In fact, we see signs of a new emerging opposition. Although the Finnish information society and the welfare state have ultimately created a basis for a new hacker ethic, historically speaking the Finns got through their survival struggles, and built their "post-survival" world of the information society and the welfare state, mainly with the help of the old Weberian Protestant ethic. This Protestant ethic continues to be the dominant Finnish work ethic: that is, seeing work as one's highest duty, in which one must do one's allotted task as well as possible, and in which suffering is even a bit noble.[12]

However, as described earlier in this book, the informational economy is driven by a different work ethic of information creation: the hacker ethic.[13] Information creators do something that they find intrinsically interesting, energizing, and even joyful. Their work is self-realization in which they use their special creative capabilities, constantly surpass themselves, and produce a creative contribution.

Of course, this conflict is much safer than the violence of civil war, but ultimately it is important for Finns because the development

[10]  Paavolainen (1966, 1967, 1971); Ylikangas (1993a,b).
[11]  Siltala (1985).
[12]  Weber (1904–5). Of course, it is well known that this "Protestant ethic" was very different from the original spirit of Luther's teachings.
[13]  Himanen (2001).

seems to be a potential source of division between workers of two sorts, in a nation that has just built itself around the information-society project. Because of the importance of this new divide we will discuss it in more detail in Chapter 8.

## The Finnish Identity

To sum up, the Finnish identity developed from the experience of a long history of survival: biological-economic survival, political-cultural survival, and even survival against the internal demons of ideologically driven violence in the first two decades of Finland's independence. The Finnish nation-state receives its legitimacy, ultimately, by delivering survival, or, to put it in another way, by guaranteeing a "post-survival" life through the information society and the welfare state. At the same time, the information society and the welfare state are not just the sources of legitimizing identity; they also build the unique Finnish identity. But, gradually, this process is questioning the survival work ethic that drove most of the development – the Protestant ethic – and suggests a more relaxed work ethic, better suited for a "post-survival" life. The Finns are now facing the hacker ethic.

Chapter 7

# THE FINNISH MODEL OF THE INFORMATION SOCIETY

Having reviewed the main features of the transformation of Finland into an information society, we try here to link them in a set of relationships that, in our view, constitute a specific Finnish model of the information society. There is no normative connotation in the use of the term "model." We use model here merely in its conceptual meaning, as a simplified representation of reality that emphasizes the key elements and their relationships in the structure and dynamics of the information society in Finland.

Before presenting the model we have built on the basis of our research, we want to introduce a disclaimer. This is not a rigorous, social-science model based on mathematical formulations and statistically measured relationships. Obviously such a methodological enterprise and data-gathering effort were beyond the limits of the intellectual exercise we have attempted in this study. We are simply presenting here an approximate, and schematic representation of our hypotheses on the dynamics of the Finnish information society, in the hope that researchers can take it up, and test these hypotheses more thoroughly, and that those interested in the Finnish information society, in Finland and in the world, can achieve a better understanding of this rich social, techno-logical, and economic experience.

Figure 7.1 describes the general model of the Finnish information society. Figures 7.2–7.4 display our submodels: the innovation and business system; the model of the relationships between state and society; and the spatial implications of the model. We will comment here on each model, without repeating the evidence and arguments that have been presented in the preceding chapters of this study.

At the heart of the Finnish model of the information society (Fig. 7.1) is a dynamic relationship between business and society, mediated by the state. What is critical in the model is the existence of dynamic feedback loops between its different elements, as indicated by our arrows. Thus, this is a self-reinforcing process that expands dynamically, if all the interactions work in the predicted direction. Some of the arrows, however, represent negative feedbacks: they are represented by a minus sign. All others assume positive relationships in the direction of the arrow. Bi-directional effects are indicated by a double arrow. Lines without an arrow denote an attribute.

Business creates wealth and fosters economic growth by increasing productivity and competitiveness in the global informational eco nomy, with its performance being ultimately measured in the stock markets. Business performance depends on its organizational restruc-turing in the form of the network enterprise, and of its capacity for technological innovation. On both counts, the IT cluster, originally structured in Finland around Nokia and other telecommunica-tions companies, is the driver of growth. However, the diffusion of networking and technological innovation to other business sectors is critical for the future evolution of the model.

The performance of Finnish business has been, and still is, supported and stimulated by the policies of the Finnish state, in its double role as a developmental state and a welfare state. On the developmental side, the state reformed the regulatory environment by deregulation, liberalization, and privatization to unleash the entrepreneurial and networking capacity of business. It also actively supported innovation, both directly through funding, and through a strengthened university system, geared toward engineering and information technology. The quality and innovativeness of the universities allowed a hacker

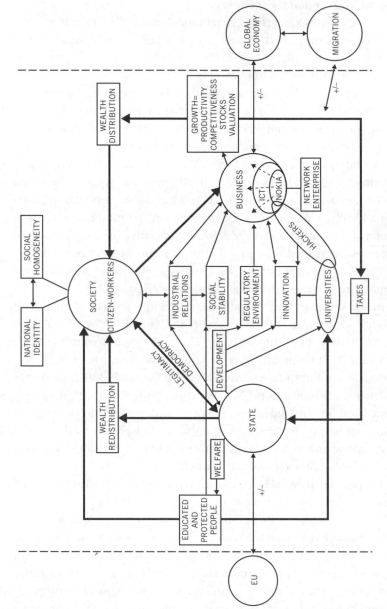

**Fig. 7.1 The Finnish model of the information society**

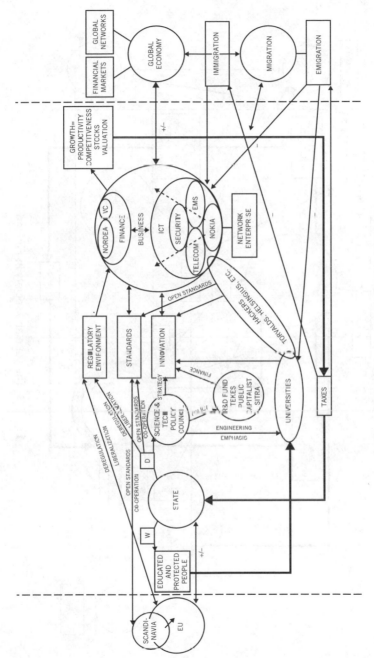

**Fig. 7.2** Business and innovation in Finland

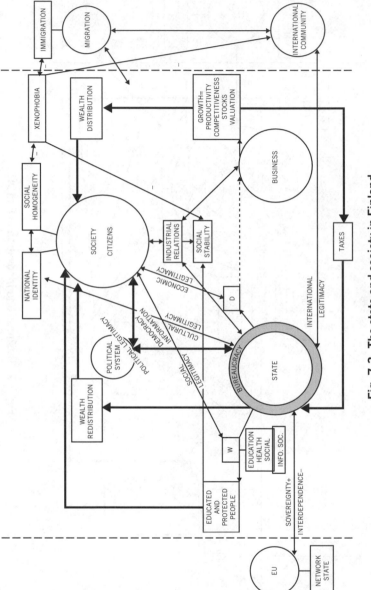

Fig. 7.3 The state and society in Finland

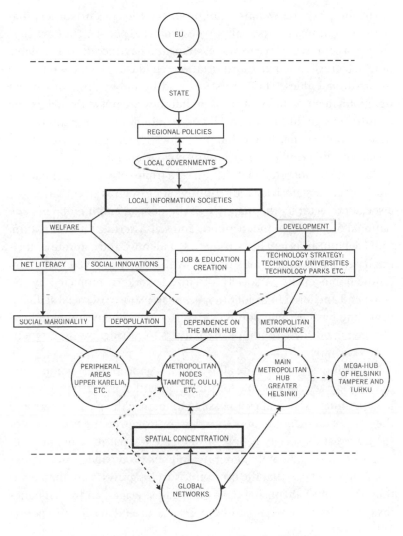

**Fig. 7.4  The spatial dimension in Finland**

culture to blossom and become an important source of innovation in Finland.

The state also contributed to a stable system of industrial relations, creating the conditions under which social partners representing capital and labor could agree on a strategy of competitiveness that would integrate workers' concerns and workers' rights.

## The Finnish Model of the Information Society

The effects of the welfare state produced the citizen/workers that are well-educated and (socially) well-protected people. They are covered by a comprehensive health system, and have access to affordable housing, efficient public transportation, child care, and a wide range of urban amenities. They are supported by public programs when unemployment or illness strikes, so that they are not at risk when the country engages in a major social and economic overhaul: this means that resistance to necessary change is much lower as the personal and social costs that could result from the change are limited.

The state is supported in its action by a triple source of legitimacy: it is a democratic state; it is a redistributive state, seen as an equalizer and a social protector by the majority of the people; and it embodies the national project of an independent and self-assertive Finnish nation. Indeed, Finnish society has strong ties of identity and communal feeling based on its history of survival, which has preserved social and ethnic homogeneity. A society of citizen/workers, protected by the state, and anchored in its identity, is a major source of social stability, providing business operations with a predictable environment, and also giving business room for maneuvers to restructure itself whenever necessary.

The legitimacy of the state allows for a regime of high taxation that most people see as favorable for their standard of living. It is this trust in government that makes it possible to finance the welfare state and the developmental state on a sound basis. However, the fiscal basis of the information society is only sustainable if what the state takes in terms of taxes ultimately generates higher productivity and higher competitiveness, so that the economic surplus grows faster than taxation, thus simultaneously increasing profits, wages, and social benefits. This is exactly what can be observed in Finland for the period 1995–2000.

At the source of this dynamic interaction is the innovation system, the quality of the labor force, and the performance of business, which together spur productivity. By using technological innovation in process and product as a driver of growth, Finland creates the material foundation for new uses of information technology based on people's social needs and projects. These new uses are the result of people-based innovation that opens new markets. Thus, the informational

146

business and the informational society feed into each other in an upward spiral of cultural creativity and wealth creation.

There are, however, three linkages with the outside world – discussed in more detail in Chapter 8 – that complicate the model. The first concerns people: on the one hand, Finland is experiencing an increasing emigration of highly entrepreneurial and skilled professionals who are escaping from high taxation and searching for broader horizons, thus diminishing the pool of human talent in Finland. On the other hand, immigration is also increasing, and may increase further, along three lines: the need for talent in the IT industries and advanced business services; the need for workers to replace an aging, stagnant population in the country; and the pressure of poor immigrants from other countries. Finland's membership in the EU will make it impossible to build a Finnish fortress isolated from the general stream of immigrants throughout Europe. These population movements, on the one hand, increase or decrease the value-adding capability of the business sector, depending on the balance of immigration/emigration. On the other hand, they decrease social homogeneity and, under conditions of xenophobia, may contribute negatively to social stability.

Second, the full integration of Finland into the global economy makes the Finnish model vulnerable to systemic volatility in the financial markets, and to the sudden, sharp downturns characteristic of the new economy.

Third, the integration of Finland into the EU creates a symbiotic and complex relationship between the Finnish state and the European network state, both enhancing and limiting the scope of government policies. Thus, on the one hand, Finland benefits from European programs supporting regional development and technological innovation. On the other hand, Finland must live in an open and competitive European environment, and will be subjected to the movements of the euro, as well as to Europe-wide regulations. Let us now examine the specific characteristics of the submodels integrated in the general model.

In the innovation and business model (Fig. 7.2) we have specified some of the key mechanisms of the Finnish developmental state. Deregulation and liberalization, starting in the 1980s, were critical steps toward creating a competitive business environment. The generation of open standards in telecommunications was decisive in positioning business and stimulating innovation. Nordic cooperation in this process, facilitated by the state and the public telecommunication operator, laid the ground for a large enough market. The universities play a major role in innovation, they are restructured and strengthened by the deliberate technology policy of the government, formed by the Science and Technology Policy Council. And the welfare state's support for university students allows hackers to practice their hackerism and thus contribute to the creation of open standards and technology innovations – and the new innovation system, the open-source model.

In modeling the relationships between state and society (Fig. 7.3) we have specified four different sources of legitimacy, on which government action is based: political legitimacy comes from the democratic state, in which the political system is the mediator between citizens and state through democratic representation and the sharing of information; social legitimacy comes from the welfare state; cultural legitimacy comes from the nationalist project underlying the Finnish state; and economic legitimacy comes from economic growth and wealth distribution from business, supported by the Finnish developmental state.

The convergence of the four processes of legitimacy provides strong social support for the Finnish state, in sharp contrast to the widespread crisis of government legitimacy in other parts of the world, including Europe. This allows the Finnish state to undertake initiatives on behalf of its citizens, and to finance these initiatives through taxation. Under the welfare state we include education, health, and social services. The information-society projects in these fields (such as advancing Internet literacy) are an important new form of the welfare state.

We also see potential breakdowns in the smooth functioning of the relationships between state and society as described in this model and explained in more detail in Chapter 8. First, within the state, the bureaucracy seems to be resisting networking, in contradiction to the potential and requirements of the informational goals of welfare applications. It also makes the workings of the welfare state less efficient and less legitimate.

Second, in the political system, the uses of information technology and networking in the relationship of the state to its citizens seem to be rather limited. Professional politicians seem to be as secluded a class in Finland as in other countries.

Third, the difficulty of Finland in coming to terms with the human dimension of globalization, that is immigration, may lead to a crisis of international legitimacy, as rising xenophobia may tarnish the current image of Finland as a humanitarian country based on principles of solidarity and the affirmation of human rights. In addition to strong national sources of legitimacy for the Finnish state, it also needs legitimacy from the international community.

Fourth, the complex relationship between shared sovereignty and relative dependency *vis-à-vis* the European network state will dominate the political debate in Finland for years to come.

Finally, the spatial dimension of the model (Fig. 7.4) includes, on the one hand, the spontaneous trends of spatial concentration and metropolitanization resulting from the clustering of innovation in the main metropolitan area connected to the global networks, that is Greater Helsinki. Potential depopulation and social marginality in rural areas and peripheral regions may follow, as well as the decline of second-tier metropolitan centers (Tampere, Turku, Oulu, Jyväskylä, Rovaniemi, and so on) *vis-à-vis* Helsinki, a challenge addressed more specifically in Chapter 8.

On the other hand, these spatial tendencies are counteracted by active projects aimed at building local/regional information societies. Some of these efforts are nationally inspired regional development policies that, when connected to local mobilization, yield considerable results, as in the growth of Oulu as a metropolitan center. Others are initiated at the grassroots, with the support of provincial governments, national institutions, and the EU, such as the exemplary Upper Karelia learning project. Still others are development efforts initiated by local governments, such as the ambitious eTampere project aimed at making Tampere a node on its own in the global networks of the information society. As a result of these counter-trends, the Finnish information society is being constituted as a highly diversified spatial and cultural society, in which the affirmation of local and regional identity leads to a diversity of models that we categorize as local information societies.

## The Finnish Model of the Information Society

The Finnish model of the information society emerged from the specific history and culture of Finland, when confronted with the global process of structural transformation. It is constrained by this global environment, and largely shaped by the characteristics of the socio-technical paradigm typical of the Information Age. However, it is uniquely shaped by the interaction between social, political, and economic actors in Finland. In this sense, it is uniquely Finnish. But this particularity does not mean that the rest of the world cannot draw important lessons for the relentless effort, under way throughout the planet, of building an information society for the benefit of humankind. As for Finland itself, the information society brings as much promise as it raises new challenges.

Chapter 8

# CONCLUSION I
# The Challenges for
# Finland

The Finnish experience shows that the Silicon Valley model is not the only way to build an advanced information society but that there is choice, the people's choice. Our analysis has pointed out some of the key characteristics of the Finnish model of the information society that differentiate it clearly from Silicon Valley or, for that matter, from Singapore, the other well-known model of an information society. Finland's special strengths include the competitive mobile companies, the state-led system of dynamic institutions advancing Finnish technology innovation, creative computer hackerism, imaginative citizen-initiated social hackerism, the combination of the information society and the welfare state from education, health to social services, local information-society initiatives, and a national identity that is technology-positive and favors networking.

However, all information societies also have their weaknesses. We have referred to some contradictions in the development of the Finnish information society in earlier chapters. The following seven challenges are in our view the most fundamental ones for Finland to address:

1. The divide between the old and the new economy.
2. The contradiction between the information society and the structures of government of the industrial age.
3. The rise of new inequalities.
4. The conflict between the current needs of the new economy and the lack of business-oriented entrepreneurialism among the young.
5. The divide between the old Protestant ethic and the hacker ethic of the information creators.
6. The vulnerability of Finland to the volatility of the global economy.
7. The contradiction between a strong national identity and integration in a multicultural world.

Let us elaborate on each challenge, individually.

## The Divide between the Old and the New Economy

The Finnish IT cluster has become the world's leading hub in the development of mobile communications technology and thus has made the Finnish economy one of the forerunners of the new economy. However, this fact hides something problematic about the structure of the Finnish new economy. The Finnish new economy is still restricted to a few sectors. After the IT cluster, the financial sector is the most economically important sector that has used information technology to transform itself creatively. The combination of information technology and some welfare uses – the formation of an e-health cluster and an e-learning cluster – is another example of a similar development. However, the integration of information technology in other industries has been remarkably slow.

The current gap between the old and the new economy can be seen from the figures showing the development of productivity by sector. The fact that productivity growth in the telecommunications sector is 25 percent and 3.5 percent in the Finnish manufacturing as a whole means that there is low productivity growth in many sectors. The transformation of these traditional sectors is one of Finland's biggest economic challenges.

In a strange way, it seems that the Finnish conception of the new economy has been both broad and narrow at the same time. Unlike many other countries, Finland has seen the combination of the welfare state and information technology as a central expression of the information society. But, at the same time, it has not been able to transform its traditional industries, which are also an important part of the new economy.

The new economy does not refer to a specific industry (e.g., the industry that creates IT products) but to an informational mode of production in different fields. And the mere use of information technology in the industry's operation or commerce does not make an industry informational. Informationalism is more than adding information technology to the existing company structures: the challenge of informationalization is the restructuring of companies on the model of the information networks, that is the transformation from an industrial company into a network enterprise. In this model, companies focus on their core competence and network with other companies with other competence based on the needs of each project. The network enterprise activates nodes in its network of suppliers, forms networks of research and development with universities and other companies, and forms task forces from its internal network of relatively autonomous units according to changing goals, which it is able to adapt in a very market-driven way based on its networking with its customers. The informational economy means the network structure in the core areas of a company's production, research and development, management, and sales. This remains a major challenge for Finland.

It seems that another important level of the concept of informationalism has not been fully realized in Finland. In the informational economy, the increasing significance of information does not mean only information that is mediated by computers but it also includes the increasing significance of the symbolic level of products: information in the sense of experiences, meanings, and identities. Of course, this level too can often be mediated by computers and thus the creation of electronic symbols – sometimes called, rather strangely, "content production" – is one of the main growth fields of the informational economy. But many times the symbolic level is not stored in a digital format. As has been mentioned, Nokia's success was partly based on its ability to be the first to transform the mobile phone from a technical device to a lifestyle tool: when one buys a Nokia phone, one actually buys a certain experience, meaning, or identity – and, as a consequence, IT companies spend more and more time in creating the symbolic level of their products as compared to mere technical development.

But, again, informationalization is not limited to the most obvious example of the IT industry. The future of very traditional fields like crafts may well lie in information creating, that is becoming creators of products with a very strong symbolic level (being handmade, stylish, original, customized, and so on). Information technology and networking can be used as it fits each case (marketing and sales, e.g., and forming networks of crafts companies). In general, when a company does not produce just commodities, goods, or routine services, but something whose design includes a strong symbolic element, then that company or person is an information creator. This can be anything ranging from creating wood furniture instead of pulp, to a farmer who does not just produce a crop but has his or her local recipes, to medical care that can integrate patients' tacit knowledge about themselves in the diagnosis and treatment. The widening of the new Finnish economy into an information economy in the broader sense represents great potential for innovation, yet its fulfillment remains a major challenge.

## The Information Society and the Industrial-Age Structures of Government

The dynamic role of the Finnish government in the Finnish innovation system was pointed out as one of its clear strengths. Also, the combination of the welfare state and the information society has begun in Finland earlier than in other countries. However, there seems to be a structural problem that is impairing Finland's progress in this area. There are very advanced goals about using information technology for welfare purposes in education, health, and social services, but the structures of implementation seem to stall these processes. We will discuss a contradiction between the informational goals and the industrial-age structures of the welfare state and the government.

Many important welfare uses of information technology have been realized and, for example, a health cluster and an e-learning cluster are forming. However, the implementation of these goals, which have made Finland exceptional in an international comparison, is moving forward so slowly that Finland threatens to lose its advantage in this area where new Nokias and a new dynamism would be possible. Most of Finland's welfare goals were already expressed at the end of 1994 but in many cases what has happened is the launch of committee after committee to write new plans, while assuming that the existing structures will take care of implementation.

The financing of the development of digital learning materials is a case in point. The bureaucratic structure of its implementation is aptly reflected in the name of the organization that is responsible for it: the Information Society Committee's Sub-Committee for Content Production. And the subcommittee is divided into seven subgroups, directed by a board of officials from eight ministries. As has been mentioned, the Information Society Committee itself was originally formed after the launch of the first national information society strategy to network expertise from the public sector, business, and research to advise the government. We continue to emphasize that one of the key factors behind Finland's strong economic and technological success has been networking. However, the difference between the networking of the Information Society Committee and the networking of the Science and Technology Policy Council is that in the first case networking has become an end in itself without a clear idea of the committee's task. The unclear status of the Information Society Committee has made it expand itself with implementation tasks, like the complicated substructure for content production. But when networking is not a dynamic means of getting something done it should be called just committee formation.

Similar structural problems have partly slowed down the implementation of other welfare technology projects like the Finnish virtual university, whose organization is very heavy, and various health projects, which have not been able to incorporate the potential of innovative business as much as they could. It seems that there is a lack of both dynamism and determination. Some more dynamic drivers outside the administration of the ministries are needed to organize the projects from content production to education and health, to avoid the situation of protecting established structures. With a focused strategic role – and a higher profile with the added representation of start-up companies, grassroots people, and university research as renewing forces – the Information Society Committee could become an important promoter of Finnish development.

This is related to the need for determination. The slow progress in the implementation of the welfare technology goals reveals a lack of belief in the significance of the goals. Many small projects have been started as such action does not require a systematic commitment. In this state of "project culture," the project people themselves often have little commitment to their goals: the small and isolated projects live and die through public funding, making them a form of social benefit. Naturally this is not enough to keep pace with the fast development of the welfare technology field in the rest of the world.

There is no denying that Finland has an exceptionally strong starting-point for succeeding in the integration of information technology and welfare expertise, as both have been its traditional strengths. However, this will require Finland to have similar innovations about the structures for advancing welfare technology as it had in advancing telecommunications technology. As with the new economy, combining the information society and the welfare state is not just a matter of using information technology for welfare purposes but about reforming the structures of the welfare state to be in line with the ideas of dynamic networking.

## The Rise of New Inequalities

Based on the available data, we concluded that Finland was able to survive the deep recession of the early 1990s with the main structures of its welfare state fundamentally unchanged. In fact, one of our key findings is that the Finnish case shows that the information society is not in contradiction with the welfare state. However, there is no denying that the new economy also creates new pressures on the Finnish idea of an equal society. We will discuss the rise of new inequalities.

The high level of unemployment that the recession created, and which still continues at around 9 percent in 2001,[1] is clearly a major concern. We have mentioned that the welfare services that were hit most during the recession were home care, psychiatric care, and help for substance abusers. Although basically the main educational, health, and social services remained as strong as before, it is worrying that the cuts made were directed at those who are least able to defend themselves: the elderly, the mentally sick, and alcoholics and drug users.

Flexible work has traditionally been resisted because it threatens to weaken the welfare state. In Finland's case there is a surprising new observation: information professionals enjoy much more protected employment than the labor force at large. This means that those who have the least need for protection have the strongest protection and those who are the most vulnerable to changes in the economy have the weakest protection. This situation is a potential source of conflict if this divide continues.

We also noted the strong pressure exerted by information-society development on the small towns and rural areas of Finland. The current development seems to be a spatial concentration in which strong nodes are becoming even stronger and weak nodes are becoming even weaker. This means spatial inequality in Finland, which is contrary to the central idea of the Finnish welfare state to provide the same opportunities everywhere in Finland. This trend seems to be worsened by the vague ideas and means of the Finnish developers of local information societies. Reversing the trend – that is, regional development – can only be based on creating jobs and education. Social inclusion in the information-society development is equally important but that does not create jobs and education by itself. Net literacy cannot be a strategy to stop the depopulation of a peripheral area, but the transformation of its old economy into a new economy, with a new

---

[1] OECD (2001b).

entrepreneurial spirit, is needed. On the other hand, just creating jobs and education does not yet guarantee social inclusion for everyone, so separate social projects in interaction with economic projects remain very important.

Yet, it may be that Finland's biggest challenge is not national but derives from the globally dominating trend of advancing economy at the cost of the welfare state. The deepening integration of the EU, based on the social models of more unequal societies, threatens the ability of Finland to retain its generous welfare state model. Without proposing a solution, Finland could clearly be active in starting a political debate on what kind of an information society, in social terms, Europeans want to build. Only by defending the combination of the information society and the welfare state in the EU, and by addressing the rise of new sources of inequality, can the Finnish welfare state continue as a genuinely inclusive model in the future.

## The Lack of Business-Oriented Entrepreneurialism among the Young

We have noted the dynamic nature of the Finnish IT cluster exemplified well by companies like Nokia or the tele-operators Sonera and Elisa. These best-known examples of Finnish information technology are also good examples of the fact that the new Finnish economy seems to be primarily driven by big old companies, unlike, for example, Silicon Valley where many of the main drivers of IT development have been start-ups (e.g., Intel, Apple, Oracle, Cisco, Sun, Netscape, Yahoo!). As entrepreneurialism is the basis of the new economy, this means that there is a contradiction between Finnish values and the kind of entrepreneurialism that its economy will need.

Finnish entrepreneurialism has been and remains at its strongest channeled through large old corporations. Nokia channeled the know-how of the spin-offs Mobira and Telefenno. Both Sonera and Elisa have acquired dozens of smaller tele-operators in their history. For all of them, simulating start-up entrepreneurialism in their own research and development laboratories has been critical – in fact, we could say that Nokia's reinvention of itself with a new and very young leadership in the 1990s was an expression of entrepreneurialism.

However, although there are new real start-up companies like SSH Communications Security and Iobox, on balance, there seems to be a deficit of start-up entrepreneurialism in the Finnish economy. Silicon Valley shows how important these kinds of start-ups are as sources of radically new technological ideas that can transform the whole industry (personal computer, Internet routers, Web browser, Internet business). It is for this reason that the low level of this type of entrepreneurialism, which is sometimes associated with strong social protection, is an important challenge for Finland. In order to renew fast enough, the innovation system needs this agile form of entrepreneurialism: people who have an idea, believe in it, and make it change the world.

One factor that will make it difficult to increase Finnish technology entrepreneurialism is the fact that Finnish development has come to a point where it is now hard to increase the number of engineers. This is because, with their current resources, the universities cannot educate more engineers than they are already doing and because, even in Finland, not all people want to be engineers.

But this might actually turn out to be fortunate because the development of the information society has also reached a point where training/skills other than engineering are becoming equally important. This does not mean solely business and marketing know-how, although they are certainly very important challenges for Finland as the lack of this orientation has been one reason for the low level of successful start-ups in Finland. It also means the social sciences, humanities, and the arts.

In fact, the challenge for Finland is not to try to have more and more engineers with the traditional financial incentives of directing university funding or tax breaks, but to encourage people to build, using their values and backgrounds, new uses for information technology, from education and health to tele-democracy and the arts or something not yet known. These can often provide great opportunities for new kinds of business entrepreneurialism. But it is also important to value non-economic forms of "entrepreneurialism": public and cultural creativity, as ends in themselves. And if information technology will not be used for the expression of all creativity, that is just healthy.

## The Protestant Ethic versus the Hacker Ethic

There is also another important challenge related to values. In our discussion of Finnish identity, we referred briefly to the traditional role of the Protestant ethic in Finnish society, which is currently being challenged by the new hacker ethic of the information creators. The Protestant ethic's idea of work as a duty is questioned by the hacker ethic's idea of a passionate and creative relation to one's work, creating an opposition between information creators and other workers.

This opposition is deepened by the dimensions of money and nationalism/globalism. As was noted, the old duty-teaching Protestant ethic made money a goal in itself, but, in the new economy, the information creators in business forget the work part of the Protestant ethic and redefine its relationship to money by elevating money higher than work: for many, the market value of the company has become more important than the profits from its work, stocks and options are becoming an important form of compensation, shadowing the salary in the case of top workers, and individuals bet on financial markets instead of just saving as the old Protestant ethic taught. As the old Protestant ethic has been particularly entrenched in Finland, this change has been especially difficult to adopt. Thus, at the moment, there seem to be two cultures competing with each other: one is the culture of cele-brating work as such and opposing the stock culture, based on Protestant arguments. The other is the culture of the new technology option millionaires, who enjoy their work and show off their wealth by driving Lamborghinis – something that is contrary to both the old Protestant ethic and the Protestant value of modesty. The divide is widened by the fact that the information creators act globally whereas the work of other workers is mostly national.

But there is also a promising third group of people who seem to mediate the opposition. The technology option millionaires do have the hacker work ethic but the original hacker relation to money is very different from theirs. Hackers in the word's true sense want to do something that they feel passionate about and in which they can realize themselves creatively, and this is their primary motivation and not the maximization of money. Hackers represent the culture of information creation without the extreme capitalism that is a dividing force in society. They also represent an important version of global thinking for Finland. Whereas the globality of business is still very much just transnationalism – cooperation between actors who are very conscious of their nationality – hackers have their national roots but often do not even know the nationality of the people they work with as they judge people on other criteria.

## The Vulnerability of Finland to the Volatility of the Global Economy

The sixth Finnish challenge is learning to live as part of a truly global economy. Finland is deeply and irreversibly within the global economy. And the global economy is characterized by systemic volatility.[2] This is because at the heart of globalization is the interdependence of financial markets electronically interconnected in real time. The size, speed, and complexity of global financial markets is unprecedented in economic history, in proportion to the economy as a whole. For instance in the United States, in 2000, the securities clearing house recorded about 100 trillion US dollars in financial transactions, that is the equivalent of more than ten times the US GDP. This predominance of financial markets is of course amplified at the scale of the world economy. Size, speed, and complexity make global markets unpredictable, thus offering ample opportunities for speculation. Furthermore, valuation in financial markets follows economic calculations only up to a point. What we call "information turbulences" from all origins also play a role in the process of financial valuation. In the Age of the Internet and other computer networks, these information turbulences are propagated throughout the world in seconds.

---

[2] See, e.g. Hutton and Giddens (2000).

## The Challenges for Finland

The net result is volatility. And because the national regulatory systems do not operate efficiently in a global financial environment, the traditional checks and controls from governments have a limited influence on the financial markets. A case in point was the failure, in October 2000, of the combined effort of the US Federal Reserve, the European Central Bank, and the Bank of Japan to stop the fall of the euro – until the markets decided otherwise. Only a global regulatory system could alleviate financial volatility to any extent, but the main economic powers, and particularly the United States, oppose such regulation; so, for the time being, volatility is a way of life for the new economy, which is highly dependent on stocks valuation. The smaller a country, the higher the potential impact on its economy of largely unpredictable, and increasingly contagious, financial crises. But Finland, as other countries, has little choice. The economy in which Finland must operate is global. And globalization means financial volatility. This is a challenge to be taken up in the day-to-day policy of the government, the strategies of companies, and people's life decisions.

We offer no solutions to this fundamental dilemma, but a few thoughts. The government could be active, within the EU, in a more deliberate push toward global financial regulation, overcoming US resistance. This will not be possible in the short term, but after a few episodes of financial danger perhaps the voices of reason will be heard. For companies, the important matter is to stay in the course, not panic, and bet on the longer-term strategy of productivity and competitiveness. Finnish society will be more patient and will survive the shocks of globalization, if it relies on a solid welfare state that provides for a basic standard of living in times of crisis. Thus, the welfare state is the best complement to globalization, not its antinomy. Globalization without security is tantamount to economic disruption and social instability. As for people, they should never reduce their life options to their stock options. Money is good, life is better, and the value of living should not depend on the value of money – which is not even a safe value, as Finland's neighbors, the Russians, who saw the value of their life savings wiped out twice in the 1990s, know. People rooted in valuing life, a welfare state guaranteeing living standards, and an economy steered in a long-term strategy of productivity growth seem to be the necessary anchors to withstand the systemic storms of the global, new economy.

## A Strong National Identity and Openness to Other Cultures

Finally, the seventh challenge that emerges from our analysis is the contradiction between strong national identity and an openness to a multicultural world. The new economy is a global economy, in which the success of a nation depends on its ability to be an attractive node for the global networks of both capital and people. And not just that: we are not merely entering a new economy but also a new society that is characterized worldwide by multiculturalism and multi-ethnicity. Finnish national identity will have to face both the economic and social challenge.

Economically, this means the ability to transform national companies into global companies and attract talent from around the world. These have been important factors in the success of Silicon Valley, where 30 percent of IT companies created in the 1990s have been founded by Indians or Chinese and numerous other companies have been started by immigrants from elsewhere.[3]

It seems that Finland has done well in the first respect: the Finnish companies have started to operate as global units and have linked themselves to the global financial markets. Finland has also attracted both foreign direct investments and stock investments in Finnish companies. However, in attracting people Finland has been much weaker.

This seems to be related to several factors. The most practical reason is the high level of taxation in Finland. It will be impossible for Finland to compete with other countries to attract talented labor with taxes at the current level. Not to mention that other countries seem to attract the top talent from Finland, including some of the brightest minds like Linus Torvalds (now in Silicon Valley) and Johan Helsingius (now working in the Netherlands).

[3] Saxenian (1999).

163

## The Challenges for Finland

Strict immigration laws are another key factor. The unwelcoming nature of Finnish immigration legislation is a reflection of the downside of a strong national identity. As was mentioned, the Finnish identity was very much shaped as a minority identity when the Finns were under the control of Sweden and Russia. The paradox is that, while Finns are now the majority in their country, they continue to behave like a minority, and as we know, minorities are not necessarily open-minded to other minorities.

In fact, if we look at the surveys of Finnish attitudes to foreigners, we get quite a bleak picture.[4] For example, 61 percent of Finns believe that "Criminality and disorder increase with foreigners," 60 percent of Finns feel that "Immigrants just want to exploit our living standards," 34 percent think that "Increasing immigration would lead to unfavorable mixing of races," and 41 percent state that "Immigration should be more limited than it is now." Only 45 percent of Finns agree with the statement "Increasing the number of foreigners working in Finland would bring positive international influences to our country." Because of these attitudes Finland remains an ethnically homogeneous country with only 2.5 percent of the population born outside Finland (as a point of comparison, the corresponding figure for California in 2000 was 25 percent).

It is true that the trend has been positive both in the figures and in the attitudes (the equivalent share of the foreign population in the mid-1980s was just 0.8 percent, and only 19 percent of Finns agreed with the statement "Increasing the number of foreigners working in Finland would bring positive international influences to our country"), but still this development is not sufficient to make Finland an attractive node for foreign talent – something that is necessary for Finland as the need for information professionals is much greater than the supply.

From the social viewpoint, Finnish attitudes toward foreigners could be a source of serious conflict with the global networks in which Finland is integrated. If xenophobic attitudes develop into a strong extreme right-wing movement or a popular nationalist party, Finland would risk its international reputation. This would make Finland not

[4] EVA (2001).

just unattractive as a country for talented people to work in but also as an investment destination (which could reflect negatively on the Finnish economy, most immediately in the stocks valuation of the Finnish companies). Xenophobic attitudes would also make European integration more painful for Finland as Europe is, and will increasingly be, a multicultural and multi-ethnic continent. In fact, the global networks in which Finland is integrated will be multicultural regardless of Finnish attitudes. Finland cannot choose a non-multicultural world but the multicultural world can choose a world without a xenophobic Finland.

So the big challenge for Finland is to see multiculturalism as a rich source of economic and cultural growth, and, in line with this, to shape itself as an attractive open node in the global networks.

Chapter 9

# CONCLUSION II
## Learning from Finland

We have emphasized that the Finnish model of the information society has been developed under specific circumstances that are not replicable as such in other contexts. However, there are a number of key analytical lessons that can be learned from this experience, and that can be a source of reflection and perhaps inspiration for other countries and regions of the world.

First, Finland shows that a fully fledged welfare state is not incompatible with technological innovation, with the development of the information society, and with a dynamic, competitive new economy. Indeed, it appears to be a decisive contributing factor to the growth of this new economy on a stable basis. It provides the human foundation for labor productivity necessary for the informational model of development, and it also brings institutional and social stability, which smoothes the damage to the economy and to people during periods of potentially sharp downturns. This welfare state is not sustainable without a high level of taxation. But taxation is not an economic problem as long as productivity and competitiveness grow faster than taxes, and as long as people recognize the benefits they receive in the form of social services and the quality of life. In this sense, Finland stands in sharp contrast to the Silicon Valley model that is entirely driven by market mechanisms, individual entrepreneurialism, and the culture of risk – with considerable social costs, acute social inequality, and a deteriorating basis for both locally generated human capital and economic infrastructure.

Second, the welfare state and cooperation between business and labor, mediated by the government, allow the development of work flexibility within a stable system of industrial relations. It shows that labor unions can accept the transformation of business practices on the condition of not having to assume an unfair share of the social costs involved in the transition to the informational model. The adaptability of Finnish employment practices, in exchange for the government coverage of social benefits and high economic growth, are in contrast with the rigidity of labor and management practices, for example, in Germany; a major obstacle in the transition of Germany to the new economy.

Third, the state has played, and continues to play, a major role in guiding economic growth and building the information society in Finland. But it has not brought the economy under bureaucratic control. Instead it has been a major liberalizer of the economic system: for example, its effort to deregulate and globalize the Finnish telecommunications sector earlier than most other European countries, was a decisive contribution to the new model of economic growth. The Finnish state has used incentives and strategic planning to complement market mechanisms, rather than substituting for them. It has also relied on participatory mechanisms, and has operated within the framework of a democratic and legitimate state. This is in contrast to the experience of Asian developmental states, which are characterized by authoritarianism in society and by a hierarchical relationship in business. The Finnish state has acted as a promoter of technological innovation, as a public venture capitalist, and a producer of knowledge labor, thus creating the conditions under which Finnish business could restructure itself and compete globally.

Moreover, the combination of deregulation and an effective state role in providing and facilitating the public infrastructure (power, facilities, telecommunication networks, transportation, housing, urban amenities, environmental preservation) has stimulated growth and avoided the gradual deterioration of this infrastructure, contrary to the situation in California, where the crisis of power supply in 2001 threatened the economic prosperity of the region. After all, electronics do need electricity. The botched deregulation of California's power supply in the 1990s has triggered an unexpected crisis in the infrastructure of the global hub of the IT revolution.

Fourth, Finland has an explicit policy to include the whole of its population in the information society. In so doing, it is developing a wide range of public uses for information technology, which ultimately result in new products and new markets. By developing information technology with a soul, Finland gives to its companies a head start in global competition, since many of the supply-driven technological gadgets developed by American and Japanese companies seem to be reaching the point of market saturation. So, Finland is an increasingly sophisticated experimental ground to gauge people's appropriation of the IT revolution, shaping the uses and markets of the next stage of the information society; especially in those uses that are based on the mobile Internet.

Fifth, spatial clustering and organizational networking of knowledge-based industries have been critical sources of productivity and competitiveness in Finland, as they have been in Silicon Valley, thus verifying once again the theory of milieux of innovation as drivers of technology and economy in the informational paradigm. But the local and regional governments in Finland have also undertaken important initiatives in diffusing technology in local societies, and in mobilizing local economies into the new techno–economic paradigm. They have been supported in their initiatives by both the national government and the European Commission, thus exemplifying the potentially dynamic role of the European network state. This is in contrast to the American experience, where devolution of power to state and local governments tends to fragment and weaken policy initiatives. The Finnish experience shows the synergy that can be created from networking between different levels of government in the design of developmental public policy.

Sixth, hackerism has been in Finland, as in the United States, a major source of technological innovation. Furthermore, by building global networks of hackerism, Finnish hackers have fully connected universities and businesses to the cutting edge of research in information technology, particularly in software. The Finnish experience, thus, confirms the importance of transboundary hackerism in cultural and technological innovation. Societies repressing hackers may be cutting off one of their major sources of intellectual capital and material wealth. But, as was shown by the example of social hackerism in Net literacy, societies can benefit from hackerism in much broader ways.

And, seventh, the Finnish experience also offers some hope for countries currently stagnating at a much lower level of development around the world. In contrast to the image of Finland as a rich, Scandinavian country, it must be remembered that only three generations ago Finland was a very poor country, with most of its population in agriculture, largely dependent on its forest resources, only loosely integrated into the main channels of capital, markets, and technology in the world, and with a very limited public coverage of people's needs. It was, overwhelmingly, a poor agrarian society surviving in harsh climatic conditions. The ability to leapfrog in about half a century from the depths of economic backwardness to the forefront of informational development shows that it is not historical fate but human effort that counts in the way societies and people improve their lives and projects.

A cultural identity and a strong national sentiment appear to be essential components of the Finnish model of the information society. They are sources of legitimacy for the active role of government, in a parallel experience to the developmental state in Asia. Identity is also projected toward the future, building Finnish pride in the collective accomplishment of Finland as an advanced information society. Social homogeneity and national solidarity strengthen the support for programs of inclusion, and favor the emergence of a society-driven model of technology use. Thus, rather than undermining global competitiveness, strong national identity provides a platform to build technological capacity and to develop social experimentation. Local and national identities add value to Finnish business and to Finnish innovators in their interaction with global networks of economy and technology.

On the other hand, the Finnish model is still largely based on social and ethnic homogeneity and on a certain reluctance to open up society to foreign influence and foreign individuals. This is in sharp contrast to the Silicon Valley experience of innovation and entrepreneurialism based on immigration and multiculturalism. If this was a lesson to retain it would be a depressing one, since xenophobia and isolationism contradict the basic values of human solidarity. Furthermore, Finland, and its imitators, will have increasing difficulty in growing and enriching themselves without looking at others, in a world increasingly interconnected, not only economically but culturally. The real lesson, we hope, is that national and cultural identity are important sources of meaning and value, but only on the condition of engaging people and countries in a multicultural dialogue based on a multi-ethnic coexistence.

# APPENDIX 1
## Flexible Work in Finland

## Table A1.1 Flexible work (absolute numbers)

| Age | 1990 | 1991 | 1992 | 1993 | 1994 | 1995 | 1996 | 1997 | 1998 | 1999 | 2000 |
|---|---|---|---|---|---|---|---|---|---|---|---|
| *Employed* | | | | | | | | | | | |
| Total **15–64** | **2 482 700** | **2 355 500** | **2 190 000** | **2 055 400** | **2 039 700** | **2 083 700** | **2 113 200** | **2 154 200** | **2 206 700** | **2 280 700** | **2 318 400** |
| 15–24 | 338 500 | 285 900 | 227 200 | 190 200 | 175 900 | 184 100 | 188 600 | 212 800 | 227 900 | 254 900 | 262 800 |
| 25–39 | 1 023 900 | 967 400 | 895 000 | 829 000 | 819 400 | 825 200 | 826 800 | 823 400 | 824 800 | 831 000 | 822 800 |
| 40–64 | 1 120 300 | 1 102 200 | 1 067 800 | 1 036 300 | 1 044 400 | 1 074 300 | 1 097 800 | 1 118 000 | 1 154 000 | 1 194 700 | 1 232 800 |
| Part-time **15–64** | **180 800** | **184 200** | **177 800** | **185 100** | **185 600** | **196 300** | **197 600** | **190 500** | **208 000** | **232 700** | **237 900** |
| 15–24 | 59 100 | 58 100 | 52 000 | 53 000 | 49 300 | 51 300 | 52 900 | 62 500 | 71 800 | 84 200 | 88 400 |
| 25–39 | 59 300 | 59 300 | 57 200 | 62 800 | 63 200 | 64 600 | 66 100 | 58 600 | 63 500 | 64 900 | 62 000 |
| 40–64 | 62 400 | 66 800 | 68 700 | 69 400 | 73 100 | 80 400 | 78 600 | 69 400 | 72 700 | 83 500 | 87 400 |
| Temporary **15–64** | | | | | | | | **338 200** | **333 400** | **332 300** | **330 900** |
| 15–24 | | | | | | | | 108 600 | 109 700 | 114 600 | 114 700 |
| 25–39 | | | | | | | | 143 700 | 136 200 | 133 400 | 130 800 |
| 40–64 | | | | | | | | 85 900 | 87 400 | 84 300 | 85 400 |
| Self-employed **15–64** | **371 300** | **347 600** | **331 200** | **316 600** | **320 300** | **312 900** | **312 600** | **308 900** | **304 600** | **308 900** | **305 900** |
| 15–24 | 20 500 | 17 100 | 16 800 | 15 700 | 14 600 | 14 200 | 13 400 | 13 000 | 11 200 | 11 500 | 10 400 |
| 25–39 | 127 800 | 115 500 | 109 300 | 105 600 | 103 900 | 99 200 | 101 200 | 96 700 | 93 800 | 92 700 | 90 300 |
| 40–64 | 222 900 | 215 000 | 205 100 | 195 300 | 201 800 | 199 400 | 198 000 | 199 200 | 199 600 | 204 800 | 205 200 |
| *ICT sectors* | | | | | | | | | | | |
| Total **15–64** | **83 200** | **80 900** | **73 500** | **69 700** | **74 200** | **85 800** | **91 000** | **93 100** | **106 400** | **118 600** | **123 400** |
| 15–24 | 11 800 | 8 000 | 5 400 | 6 300 | 6 200 | 9 000 | 8 700 | 10 900 | 13 200 | 15 100 | 16 100 |
| 25–39 | 42 900 | 41 500 | 37 800 | 33 800 | 39 000 | 44 900 | 47 300 | 48 000 | 54 200 | 60 000 | 63 700 |
| 40–64 | 28 500 | 31 400 | 30 300 | 29 500 | 29 000 | 31 800 | 35 100 | 34 200 | 39 000 | 43 600 | 43 600 |
| Part-time **15–64** | **2 500** | **2 200** | **2 000** | **2 100** | **2 100** | **3 200** | **2 600** | **3 300** | **4 500** | **5 600** | **6 200** |
| 15–24 | 1 000 | 500 | 400 | 700 | 700 | 900 | 800 | 1 400 | 1 900 | 2 600 | 3 200 |
| 25–39 | 1 000 | 900 | 900 | 1 000 | 900 | 1 300 | 1 300 | 1 200 | 1 500 | 1 700 | 1 500 |
| 40–64 | 500 | 800 | 700 | 400 | 500 | 1 100 | 600 | 700 | 1 000 | 1 300 | 1 500 |

| Category | Age | | | | | | | | | | | |
|---|---|---|---|---|---|---|---|---|---|---|---|---|
| Temporary | 15–64 | | | | | | | | 10 100 | 11 300 | 12 200 | 11 700 |
| | 15–24 | | | | | | | | 4 700 | 5 800 | 6 600 | 6 200 |
| | 25–39 | | | | | | | | 4 200 | 4 400 | 4 400 | 4 700 |
| | 40–64 | | | | | | | | 1 300 | 1 200 | 1 200 | 900 |
| Self-employed | 15–64 | 2 900 | 3 400 | 2 400 | 2 700 | 3 600 | 4 100 | 4 400 | 3 900 | 3 900 | 5 000 | 5 300 |
| | 15–24 | 200 | 200 | 0 | 100 | 100 | 100 | 300 | 200 | 500 | 500 | 300 |
| | 25–39 | 1 400 | 1 500 | 1 100 | 1 200 | 1 500 | 1 900 | 2 200 | 1 600 | 1 400 | 1 700 | 2 000 |
| | 40–64 | 1 300 | 1 700 | 1 300 | 1 400 | 2 000 | 2 100 | 1 800 | 2 100 | 2 100 | 2 800 | 3 000 |
| *Information professionals* Total | 15–64 | 149 700 | 141 700 | 129 900 | 125 500 | 126 800 | 136 800 | 142 500 | 147 100 | 158 600 | 178 400 | 187 500 |
| | 15–24 | 21 900 | 14 300 | 10 300 | 9 400 | 7 800 | 11 400 | 11 000 | 14 100 | 16 200 | 19 400 | 22 800 |
| | 25–39 | 76 900 | 73 400 | 64 900 | 63 200 | 65 300 | 68 800 | 70 500 | 71 500 | 75 700 | 83 800 | 86 500 |
| | 40–64 | 50 900 | 54 000 | 54 700 | 52 800 | 53 600 | 56 700 | 61 000 | 61 600 | 66 700 | 75 200 | 78 200 |
| Part-time | 15–64 | 5 500 | 4 600 | 4 400 | 5 100 | 4 600 | 5 900 | 5 000 | 5 900 | 6 700 | 9 000 | 9 900 |
| | 15–24 | 2 300 | 1 300 | 900 | 1 600 | 900 | 1 200 | 1 200 | 2 400 | 2 900 | 3 600 | 4 600 |
| | 25–39 | 2 100 | 2 100 | 2 100 | 2 400 | 2 400 | 2 600 | 2 300 | 2 000 | 2 400 | 3 100 | 2 500 |
| | 40–64 | 1 200 | 1 200 | 1 400 | 1 100 | 1 400 | 2 100 | 1 500 | 1 500 | 1 500 | 2 300 | 2 800 |
| Temporary | 15–64 | | | | | | | | 18 200 | 19 100 | 20 600 | 21 300 |
| | 15–24 | | | | | | | | 7 100 | 8 200 | 9 400 | 9 500 |
| | 25–39 | | | | | | | | 8 200 | 8 400 | 8 400 | 8 600 |
| | 40–64 | | | | | | | | 2 900 | 2 500 | 2 800 | 3 200 |
| Self-employed | 15–64 | 7 200 | 8 500 | 7 500 | 7 400 | 8 300 | 9 100 | 9 000 | 8 600 | 9 300 | 11 500 | 12 100 |
| | 15–24 | 400 | 300 | 200 | 200 | 100 | 300 | 300 | 500 | 700 | 700 | 500 |
| | 25–39 | 3 400 | 3 700 | 3 500 | 3 600 | 3 900 | 3 900 | 3 700 | 3 300 | 3 600 | 4 100 | 3 900 |
| | 40–64 | 3 400 | 4 500 | 3 800 | 3 700 | 4 200 | 4 900 | 5 000 | 4 900 | 4 900 | 6 800 | 7 700 |

**Table A1.2  Share of flexible work (percent)**

| | Age | 1990 | 1991 | 1992 | 1993 | 1994 | 1995 | 1996 | 1997 | 1998 | 1999 | 2000 |
|---|---|---|---|---|---|---|---|---|---|---|---|---|
| *Employed* | **15–64** | **22.2** | **22.6** | **23.2** | **24.4** | **24.8** | **24.4** | **24.1** | **38.9** | **38.3** | **38.3** | **37.7** |
| Total flexible | 15–24 | 23.5 | 26.3 | 30.3 | 36.1 | 36.3 | 35.6 | 35.2 | 86.5 | 84.6 | 82.5 | 81.2 |
| | 25–39 | 18.3 | 18.1 | 18.6 | 20.3 | 20.4 | 19.8 | 20.2 | 36.3 | 35.6 | 35.0 | 34.4 |
| | 40–64 | 25.5 | 25.6 | 25.6 | 25.5 | 26.3 | 26.0 | 25.2 | 31.7 | 31.2 | 31.2 | 30.7 |
| Part-time | **15–64** | **7.3** | **7.8** | **8.1** | **9.0** | **9.1** | **9.4** | **9.4** | **8.8** | **9.4** | **10.2** | **10.3** |
| | 15–24 | 17.5 | 20.3 | 22.9 | 27.9 | 28.0 | 27.9 | 28.0 | 29.4 | 31.5 | 33.0 | 33.6 |
| | 25–39 | 5.8 | 6.1 | 6.4 | 7.6 | 7.7 | 7.8 | 8.0 | 7.1 | 7.7 | 7.8 | 7.5 |
| | 40–64 | 5.6 | 6.1 | 6.4 | 6.7 | 7.0 | 7.5 | 7.2 | 6.2 | 6.3 | 7.0 | 7.1 |
| Temporary | **15–64** | | | | | | | | **15.7** | **15.1** | **14.6** | **14.3** |
| | 15–24 | | | | | | | | 51.0 | 48.1 | 45.0 | 43.6 |
| | 25–39 | | | | | | | | 17.5 | 16.5 | 16.1 | 15.9 |
| | 40–64 | | | | | | | | 7.7 | 7.6 | 7.1 | 6.9 |
| Self-employed | **15–64** | **15.0** | **14.8** | **15.1** | **15.4** | **15.7** | **15.0** | **14.8** | **14.3** | **13.8** | **13.5** | **13.2** |
| | 15–24 | 6.1 | 6.0 | 7.4 | 8.3 | 8.3 | 7.7 | 7.1 | 6.1 | 4.9 | 4.5 | 4.0 |
| | 25–39 | 12.5 | 11.9 | 12.2 | 12.7 | 12.7 | 12.0 | 12.2 | 11.7 | 11.4 | 11.2 | 11.0 |
| | 40–64 | 19.9 | 19.5 | 19.2 | 18.8 | 19.3 | 18.6 | 18.0 | 17.8 | 17.3 | 17.1 | 16.6 |

| | | | | | | | | | | | |
|---|---|---|---|---|---|---|---|---|---|---|---|
| *ICT sectors* | | | | | | | | | | | |
| Total flexible **15–64** | **6.5** | **6.9** | **6.0** | **6.9** | **7.7** | **8.5** | **7.7** | **18.6** | **18.5** | **19.2** | **18.8** |
| 15–24 | 10.2 | 8.8 | 7.4 | 12.7 | 12.9 | 11.1 | 12.6 | 57.8 | 62.1 | 64.2 | 60.2 |
| 25–39 | 5.6 | 5.8 | 5.3 | 6.5 | 6.2 | 7.1 | 7.4 | 14.6 | 13.5 | 13.0 | 12.9 |
| 40–64 | 6.3 | 8.0 | 6.6 | 6.1 | 8.6 | 10.1 | 6.8 | 12.0 | 11.0 | 12.2 | 12.4 |
| Part-time **15–64** | **3.0** | **2.7** | **2.7** | **3.0** | **2.8** | **3.7** | **2.9** | **3.5** | **4.2** | **4.7** | **5.0** |
| 15–24 | 8.5 | 6.3 | 7.4 | 11.1 | 11.3 | 10.0 | 9.2 | 12.8 | 14.4 | 17.2 | 19.9 |
| 25–39 | 2.3 | 2.2 | 2.4 | 3.0 | 2.3 | 2.9 | 2.7 | 2.5 | 2.8 | 2.8 | 2.4 |
| 40–64 | 1.8 | 2.5 | 2.3 | 1.4 | 1.7 | 3.5 | 1.7 | 2.0 | 2.6 | 3.0 | 3.4 |
| Temporary **15–64** | | | | | | | | **10.8** | **10.6** | **10.3** | **9.5** |
| 15–24 | | | | | | | | 43.1 | 43.9 | 43.7 | 38.5 |
| 25–39 | | | | | | | | 8.8 | 8.1 | 7.3 | 7.4 |
| 40–64 | | | | | | | | 3.8 | 3.1 | 2.8 | 2.1 |
| Self-employed **15–64** | **3.5** | **4.2** | **3.3** | **3.9** | **4.9** | **4.8** | **4.8** | **4.2** | **3.7** | **4.2** | **4.3** |
| 15–24 | 1.7 | 2.5 | 0.0 | 1.6 | 1.6 | 1.1 | 3.4 | 1.8 | 3.8 | 3.3 | 1.9 |
| 25–39 | 3.3 | 3.6 | 2.9 | 3.6 | 3.8 | 4.2 | 4.7 | 3.3 | 2.6 | 2.8 | 3.1 |
| 40–64 | 4.6 | 5.4 | 4.3 | 4.7 | 6.9 | 6.6 | 5.1 | 6.1 | 5.4 | 6.4 | 6.9 |
| *Information professionals* | | | | | | | | | | | |
| Total flexible **15–64** | **8.5** | **9.2** | **9.2** | **10.0** | **10.2** | **11.0** | **9.8** | **22.2** | **22.1** | **23.0** | **23.1** |
| 15–24 | 12.3 | 11.2 | 10.7 | 19.1 | 12.8 | 13.2 | 13.6 | 70.9 | 72.8 | 70.6 | 64.0 |
| 25–39 | 7.2 | 7.9 | 8.6 | 9.5 | 9.6 | 9.4 | 8.5 | 18.9 | 19.0 | 18.6 | 17.3 |
| 40–64 | 9.0 | 10.6 | 9.5 | 9.1 | 10.4 | 12.3 | 10.7 | 15.1 | 13.3 | 15.8 | 17.5 |

**Table A1.2 Continued**

| | Age | 1990 | 1991 | 1992 | 1993 | 1994 | 1995 | 1996 | 1997 | 1998 | 1999 | 2000 |
|---|---|---|---|---|---|---|---|---|---|---|---|---|
| Part-time | **15–64** | **3.7** | **3.2** | **3.4** | **4.1** | **3.6** | **4.3** | **3.5** | **4.0** | **4.2** | **5.0** | **5.3** |
| | 15–24 | 10.5 | 9.1 | 8.7 | 17.0 | 11.5 | 10.5 | 10.9 | 17.0 | 17.9 | 18.6 | 20.2 |
| | 25–39 | 2.7 | 2.9 | 3.2 | 3.8 | 3.7 | 3.8 | 3.3 | 2.8 | 3.2 | 3.7 | 2.9 |
| | 40–64 | 2.4 | 2.2 | 2.6 | 2.1 | 2.6 | 3.7 | 2.5 | 2.4 | 2.2 | 3.1 | 3.6 |
| Temporary | **15–64** | | | | | | | | **12.4** | **12.0** | **11.5** | **11.4** |
| | 15–24 | | | | | | | | 50.4 | 50.6 | 48.5 | 41.7 |
| | 25–39 | | | | | | | | 11.5 | 11.1 | 10.0 | 9.9 |
| | 40–64 | | | | | | | | 4.7 | 3.7 | 3.7 | 4.1 |
| Self-employed | **15–64** | **4.8** | **6.0** | **5.8** | **5.9** | **6.5** | **6.7** | **6.3** | **5.8** | **5.9** | **6.4** | **6.5** |
| | 15–24 | 1.8 | 2.1 | 1.9 | 2.1 | 1.3 | 2.6 | 2.7 | 3.5 | 4.3 | 3.6 | 2.2 |
| | 25–39 | 4.4 | 5.0 | 5.4 | 5.7 | 6.0 | 5.7 | 5.2 | 4.6 | 4.8 | 4.9 | 4.5 |
| | 40–64 | 6.7 | 8.3 | 6.9 | 7.0 | 7.8 | 8.6 | 8.2 | 8.0 | 7.3 | 9.0 | 9.8 |

# APPENDIX 2
## The Spatial Distribution of Internet Domains in Finland

**Table A2.1 Domains by regional councils**

| Regional council | gTLD | fiTLD | allTLD |
|---|---|---|---|
| Uusimaa | 30 990 | 15 212 | 46 202 |
| Pirkanmaa | 3 940 | 2 190 | 6 130 |
| Varsinais-Suomi | 3 230 | 2 357 | 5 587 |
| North Ostrobothnia | 1 960 | 1 099 | 3 059 |
| Satakunta | 1 170 | 893 | 2 063 |
| Central Finland | 940 | 1 051 | 1 991 |
| South Karelia | 1 450 | 414 | 1 864 |
| Ostrobothnia | 940 | 732 | 1 672 |
| Kanta-Häme | 1 020 | 595 | 1 615 |
| Päijät-Häme | 760 | 852 | 1 612 |
| North Savo | 690 | 783 | 1 473 |
| South Ostrobothnia | 510 | 668 | 1 178 |
| Kymenlaakso | 540 | 587 | 1 127 |
| South Savo | 610 | 471 | 1 081 |
| Lapland | 590 | 478 | 1 068 |
| North Karelia | 600 | 457 | 1 057 |
| East Uusimaa | 460 | 387 | 847 |
| Kainuu | 520 | 211 | 731 |
| Central Ostrobothnia | 120 | 185 | 305 |
| Åland | 110 | 62 | 172 |

Table A2.2 Domains by top postal codes

| Postal | Municipality | Regional council | allTLD domains |
|--------|--------------|------------------|----------------|
| 0010 | Helsinki | Uusimaa | 5 846 |
| 0130 | Vantaa | Uusimaa | 5 388 |
| 0058 | Helsinki | Uusimaa | 3 190 |
| 3310 | Tampere | Pirkanmaa | 2 030 |
| 2010 | Turku | Varsinais-Suomi | 1 572 |
| 0015 | Helsinki | Uusimaa | 1 526 |
| 5310 | Lappeenranta | Etelä-Karjala | 1 435 |
| 0012 | Helsinki | Uusimaa | 1 236 |
| 0213 | Espoo | Uusimaa | 1 160 |
| 0018 | Helsinki | Uusimaa | 1 099 |
| 0017 | Helsinki | Uusimaa | 854 |
| 0051 | Helsinki | Uusimaa | 824 |
| 0013 | Helsinki | Uusimaa | 733 |
| 0216 | Espoo | Uusimaa | 656 |
| 9110 | Ii | Pohjois-Pohjanmaa | 580 |
| 0021 | Helsinki | Uusimaa | 565 |
| 2810 | Pori | Satakunta | 565 |
| 0053 | Helsinki | Uusimaa | 549 |
| 0210 | Espoo | Uusimaa | 549 |
| 3321 | Tampere | Pirkanmaa | 534 |
| 0162 | Vantaa | Uusimaa | 519 |
| 0215 | Espoo | Uusimaa | 519 |
| 8710 | Kajaani | Kainuu | 504 |
| 0145 | Vantaa | Uusimaa | 488 |
| 0039 | Helsinki | Uusimaa | 473 |
| 0038 | Helsinki | Uusimaa | 458 |
| 0050 | Helsinki | Uusimaa | 458 |
| 5010 | Mikkeli | Etelä-Savo | 443 |
| 6510 | Vaasa | Pohjanmaa | 443 |
| 9010 | Oulu | Pohjois-Pohjanmaa | 443 |
| 0025 | Helsinki | Uusimaa | 412 |
| 0014 | Helsinki | Uusimaa | 397 |
| 3320 | Tampere | Pirkanmaa | 397 |
| 0221 | Espoo | Uusimaa | 382 |

**Table A2.2** Continued

| Postal | Municipality | Regional council | allTLD domains |
|--------|--------------|------------------|----------------|
| 1110 | Riihimäki | Kanta-Häme | 382 |
| 0026 | Helsinki | Uusimaa | 366 |
| 0020 | Helsinki | Uusimaa | 351 |
| 0056 | Helsinki | Uusimaa | 351 |
| 0024 | Helsinki | Uusimaa | 336 |
| 0220 | Espoo | Uusimaa | 336 |
| 0228 | Espoo | Uusimaa | 336 |
| 0232 | Espoo | Uusimaa | 336 |
| 0234 | Espoo | Uusimaa | 336 |
| 0236 | Espoo | Uusimaa | 336 |
| 2052 | Turku | Varsinais-Suomi | 336 |

# Bibliography

Abbate, Janet (1999) *Inventing the Internet*. Cambridge, MA: MIT Press.

Academy of Finland (2001) "1990-luvun talouskriisi -tutkimusohjelma" (The Economic Crisis of the 1990s Research Program). http://www. aka.fi/index.cfm?main_frame=http://www.aka.fi/users/70/373.cfm.

Alapuro, Risto (1994) *Suomen synty paikallisena ilmiönä 1890–1933* (The Birth of Finland as a Local Phenomenon 1890–1933). Porvoo: Hanki ja jää.

Alasuutari, Pertti and Ruuska, Petri (eds) (1998) *Elävänä Euroopassa: Muuttuva suomalainen identiteetti* (Living in Europe: Changing Finnish Identity), Sitra 210. Tampere: Vastapaino.

Ali-Yrkkö, Jyrki (2001) *Nokia's Network: Gaining Competitiveness from Co-operation*, Etla series B, 174. Helsinki: Taloustieto.

—— Paija, Laura, Reilly, Catherine, and Ylä-Anttila, Pekka (2000) *Nokia: A Big Company in a Small Country*, Etla series B, 162. Helsinki: Taloustieto.

Anttiroiko, Ari-Veikko (1999a) *The Informational Region: Promoting Regional Development in the Information Age*. Tampere: University of Tampere, Department of Local Government Studies.

—— (1999b) *Making Sense of Information Society Strategy: A Critical Review of IS Strategies at National, Regional and Local Levels in Finland*. Tampere: University of Tampere, Department of Local Government Studies, publication series 3.

—— and Savolainen, Reijo (1999) "The Role of Local Government in Promoting IS Development in Finland," *Finnish Local Government Studies*, 3.

Apo, Satu and Ehrnrooth, Jari (1996) *Millaisia olemme? Puheenvuoroja suomalaisista mentaliteeteista* (What are We Like? Perspectives on Finnish Mentalities). Helsinki: Kunnallisalan kehittämissäätiö.

Archibugi, D. and Lundvall, B-Å. (eds) (2001) *The Globalising Learning Economy*. Oxford: Oxford University Press.

# Bibliography

Asplund, Rita (ed.) (2000) *Public R&D Funding, Technological Competitiveness, Productivity, and Job Creation*, Etla series B, 168. Helsinki: Taloustieto.

Aula, Pekka and Oksanen, Antti (2000) *eEpos:suomalainen Internet-unelma* (E-pos: The Finnish Internet Dream). Helsinki: WSOY.

Berners-Lee, Tim (1999) *Weaving the Web: The Original Design and Ultimate Destiny of the World Wide Web by its Inventor*. New York: HarperCollins.

von Bonsdorff, Lars (1965) *Nokia Aktiebolag 1865–1965* (Nokia Inc.). Helsinki.

Bratt, Christian (1996) *Labor Relations in 18 Countries*. Stockholm: Swedish Employers' Confederation.

Bruun, Staffan and Wallén, Mosse (2000) *Boken om Nokia* (A Book on Nokia). Stockholm: Fischer and Co.

Brynjolffson, E. (1997) "Information Technology and the Reorganization of Work," paper presented to the Conference on "Vernetzung als Wettbewerbsfaktor," Johann Wolfgang Goethe Universitat, Frankfurt, September 4.

Buderi, Robert (2000) "Funding Central Research", *Research Technology Management*, 43 (4).

Cahalan, Margaret Werner (1986) *Historical Corrections Statistics in the United States, 1850–1984*. Washington, DC: Department of Justice.

Carnoy, Martin (2000) *Sustaining the New Economy: Work, Family, and Community in the Information Age*. Cambridge, MA: Harvard University Press.

Castells, Manuel (1999) "The Culture of Cities in the Information Age," paper presented to the Library of Congress Conference "Frontiers of the Mind in the Twenty-first Century," Washington DC, June 14–18, 1999. Reprinted in Ida Susser (ed.) (2001) *The Castells Reader on Cities and Social Theory*, pp. 367–89, Oxford: Blackwell.

—— (2000a) *The Information Age: Economy, Society and Culture*, 2nd edn, 3 vols. Oxford: Blackwell.

—— (2000b) "Materials for an Exploratory Theory of the Network Society," *British Journal of Sociology*, 1.

—— and Hall, Peter (1994) *Technopoles of the World: The Making of 21st Century Industrial Complexes*. London: Routledge.

—— Goh, Lee, and Kwok, Reginald (1990) *The Shek Kip Mei Syndrome: Economic Development and Public Housing in Hong Kong and Singapore*. London: Pion.

Coogan, K. and Kangas, S. (2001) *Nuoret ja Kommunikaatioakrobatia: 16–18 vuotiaiden kännykkä- ja internetkulttuurit* (The Communication Acrobatics

**Bibliography**

of the Young: The Mobile and Internet Cultures of 16–18 year olds). Helsinki: Elisa Communications.

Council of State (1985) *Reports by the Council of State to Parliament on Finland's Science and Technology Policy*, September 12. Helsinki.

—— (1993) *Suomi 2020: Visioita kansakunnan tulevaisuudesta* (Finland 2020: Visions of the Nation's Future). Valtioneuvosten selonteko eduskunnalle pitkän aikavälin tulevaisuudesta, Valtioneuvoston kanslian julkaisusarja 1. Helsinki: Painatuskeskus.

—— (1995a) *Developing a Finnish Information Society: Decision in Principle.* Helsinki.

—— (1995b) *Government Programme*, April 13, www.vn. fi/vn/english/government1995/vn14e.htm.

—— (1997) *Reilu ja rohkea – vastuun ja osaamisen Suomi* (Fair and Bold: Responsible and Knowledgeable Finland), Government Report on the Future to Parliament. Helsinki: Valtioneuvoston kanslia.

—— (1999) *Government Programme*, April 15, http://www. vn.fi/vn/english/vn14e.htm.

—— (2001) *Government's Project Portfolio*, February 7, http:// www.vn.fi/ vn/suomi/julkaisu/salkku1_2001.pdf.

Cronström, Eige and Ström, Holger (1965) *Puoli vuosisataa kaapeliteollisuutta 1912–1962* (Fifty Years of Cablework 1912–1962). Helsinki: Suomen Kaapelitehdas Oy.

Deininger, Klaus and Squire, Lyn (1996) *A New Data Set Measuring Income Inequality.* Washington, DC: World Bank (http://www.worldbank. org/research/growth/dddeisqu.htm).

Edquist, C. (ed.) (1997) *Systems of Innovation: Technologies, Institutions and Organizations.* London: Pinter.

Ekman, Karl (1929) *Nokia bruk 1868–1929* (Nokia Factory 1868–1929). Helsinki.

Esping-Andersen, Gosta (1990) *The Three Worlds of Welfare Capitalism.* Oxford: Oxford University Press.

Etla (2001) *Productivity Growth and Micro-level Restructuring: Finnish Experiences during the Turbulent Decades.* Helsinki: Etla.

EVA (Elinkeinoelämän valtuuskunta) (2001) *Erilaisuuksien Suomi: Raportti suomalaisten asenteista* (The Finland of Differences: A Report on Finnish Attitudes), Helsinki, http://www.eva.fi/julkaisut/raportit/asenne2001/ sisallys.htm.

Fischer, Claude (1992) *America Calling: A Social History of the Telephone to 1940.* Berkeley, CA: University of California Press.

Freedom House (2001) *Press Freedom Survey 2001*, New York, http://www. freedomhouse.org/pfs2001/pfs2001.pdf.

Freeman, C. (1987) *Technology Policy and Economic Performance: Lessons from Japan*. London: Pinter.

Ganivet, Angel (1905) *Cartas Finlandesas*.

Gillies, James and Cailliau, Robert (2000) *How the Web was Born: The Story of the World Wide Web*. Oxford: Oxford University Press.

Graham, Stephen and Marvin, Simon (2001) *Splintering Urbanism*. London: Routledge.

Haatanen, Pekka (1992) "Suomalaisen hyvinvointivaltion kehitys," in Olavi Riihinen (ed.), *Sosiaalipolitiikka 2017: Näkökulmia suomalaisen yhteiskunnan kehitykseen ja tulevaisuuteen* (Social Policy 2017), Sitra 123. Porvoo: WSOY.

—— and Suonoja, Kyösti (1992) *Suuriruhtinaskunnasta hyvinvointivaltioon: Sosiaali- ja terveysministeriö 75 vuotta* (From a Grand Duchy to a Welfare State). Helsinki: VAPK.

Häikiö, Martti (1995) *Reikäkorttimodeemista Tiedon Valtatielle: Suomen datasiirron historia*. Helsinki: Datatie.

—— (1998) *Alkuräjähdys: Radiolinja ja Suomen GSM-matkapuhelintoiminta 1988–1998* (Big Bang: Radiolinja and the Finnish GSM Business 1988–1998). Helsinki: Edita.

—— (2001) *Nokia Oyj:n historia*, 3 vols. Helsinki: Edita (forthcoming in English as *History of Nokia Corporation*, 2001).

Häkkinen, Antti (ed.) (1992) *Just a Sack of Potatoes?: Crisis Experiences in European Societies*. Helsinki: Suomen historiallinen seura.

Hammer, M. and Champy, J. (1993) *Re-engineering the Corporation*. New York: The Free Press.

Hannula, Mika (1997) *Suomi, suomalaisuus, olla suomalainen: 21 henkilöhaastattelua ja näkökulmaa suomalaisuudesta* (Finland, Finnishness, to be a Finn). Helsinki: Like.

Hein, Irene (ed.) (1998) *Tieto- ja viestintätekniikka elinikäisen oppimisen apuna* (ICT as a Tool in Life-long Learning). Tieto- ja viestintätekniikka opetuksessa ja oppimisessa, Report 4, Sitra 192. Helsinki: Sitra.

Held, David, McGrew, Anthony, Goldblatt, David, and Perraton, Jonathan (1999) *Global Transformations: Politics, Economics and Culture*. Stanford, CA: Stanford University Press.

HEX (2002) "Market Capitalisation and Number of Listed Companies", http://www.hex.fi/pdf/slide6.pdf.

Himanen, Pekka (2001) *The Hacker Ethic and the Spirit of the Information Age* (prologue by Linus Torvalds and epilogue by Manuel Castells). New York: Random House.

# Bibliography

von Hofer, Hans (1997) *Nordic Criminal Statistics 1950–1995.* Stockholm: Stockholm University.

Hoving, Victor (1948) *Suomen Gummitehdas Osakeyhtiö 1898–1948* (The Finnish Rubber Factory 1898–1948). Helsinki.

Huovinen, Liisa (ed.) (1998) *Peruskoulujen, lukioiden, ammatillisten oppilaitosten ja varhaiskasvatuksen nykytilanne ja tulevaisuudennäkymat* (The State and Future Prospects of Comprehensive Schools, High Schools, Vocational Institutions, and Early Education). Tieto- ja viestintätekniikka opetuksessa ja oppimisessa, Report 3, Sitra 191. Helsinki: Sitra.

Hutton, Will and Giddens, Anthony (2000) *On the Edge: Living with Global Capitalism.* London: Jonathan Cape.

IDC (International Data Corporation) (1996–2001) *The IDC/World Times Information Society Index.*

Imai, Ken'ichi (1990) *Joho netto waku shakai no tenbo* (The Information Network Society). Tokyo: Chikuma Shobo.

IMD (International Institute for Management Development) (2001) *The World Competitiveness Yearbook 2001.* Lausanne: IMD.

Järvinen, Hannu-Matti (1994) "Re: Verkkohistoriikit" (Re: Net Histories) (sfnet.tietoliikenne), 15 March.

Jussila, Osmo (1987) *Maakunnasta valtioksi: Suomen valtion synty* (From a Province to a State: The Birth of Finland as a State). Porvoo: WSOY.

Jutikkala, Eino (1958) *Suomen talonpojan historia* (A History of the Finnish Peasant). Suomalaisen Kirjallisuuden Seuran toimituksia 257. Helsinki: Suomalaisen kirjallisuuden seura.

Kajander, Ani, Leppo, Anja, Taipale, Vappu, and Valtonen, Hannu (1994) "Hyvinvointiklusteri – tiedolle rakennettu" (Well-being Cluster – Built on Knowledge), *Suomi tietoyhteiskunnaksi – kansalliset linjaukset,* Appendix Report 1: *Strategian perustelumuistiot,* December.

Kalela, Jorma, Kiander, Jaakko, Kivikuru, Ullamaija, Loikkanen, Heikki, and Simpura, Jussi (eds) (2001) *Down from the Heavens, Up from the Ashes: The Finnish Economic Crisis of the 1990s in the Light of Economic and Social Research.* Helsinki: Valtion taloudellinen tutkimuskeskus (Government Institute for Economic Research).

Kangasharju, Aki, Laakso, Seppo, Loikkanen, Heikki, Riihelä, Marja, and Sullström, Risto (2001) "Economic Crisis of the 1990s: What Happened to Regional Convergence and Inequality, and Housing Market Phenomena in Boom and Bust?" in Jarma Kalela *et al.* (eds) (2001) *Down from the Heavens, Up from the Ashes: The Finnish Economic Crisis of the 1990s in the Light of Economic and Social Research.* Helsinki: Valtion taloudellinen tutkimuskeskus (Government Institute for Economic Research).

# Bibliography

Käpyaho, Juhani (1996) *Tieteen tietokoneet ja tietoyhteydet* (The Computers and Networks of Science). Helsinki: CSC – Tieteellinen laskenta oy.

Kasesniemi, Eija-Liisa and Rautiainen, Pirjo (2001) *Kännyssä piilevät sanomat: Nuoret, väline ja viesti.* Tampere: Tampere University Press.

Kasvio, Antti (2001) "Nokia and the New Economy", University of Tampere, www.info.uta.fi/winsoc/engl/lect/NOKIA.htm.

Kautto, Mikko, Fritzell, Johan, Hvinden, Björn, Kvist, Jon, and Uusitalo, Hannu (2001) *Nordic Welfare States in the European Context.* London: Routledge.

Ketamo, H., Vasama, J. and Multisilta, J. (2000a) *Lasten ja nuorten matkaviestinnän käyttötilanteet.* Turku: Turun yliopisto, Rauman opettajankoulutuslaitos, Porin korkeakouluyksikkö.

—— —— —— (2000b) *Matkaviestinnän käyttö lasten ja nuorten keskuudessa.* Turku: Turun yliopisto, Rauman opettajankoulutuslaitos, Porin korkeakouluyksikkö.

Kivi, Aleksis (1991) *The Seven Brothers,* trans. Richard A. Impola. New Paltz, NY: Finnish American Translators Association.

Klinge, Matti (1991) *Let us be Finns.* Helsinki: Otava.

—— (1993) *The Finnish Tradition: Essays on Structures and Identities in the North of Europe.* Helsinki: Suomen historiallinen seura.

Kohi, Pertti (1976) *Technology Assessment.* Helsinki: Sitra.

Koivukangas, Pirjo and Valtonen, Hannu (eds) (1995a) *Oulun seudun hyvinvointiklusteri* (The Oulu Region Well-being Cluster), Stakes aiheita 33. Helsinki: Stakes.

—— —— (1995b) *Hyvinvointiklusteri: Sosiaali- ja terveydenhuollon palvelujärjestelmän, teollisuuden ja tutkimuksen verkko* (The Well-being Cluster: A Network of the Health and Social Service System, Industry, and Research), Stakes Reports 181. Helsinki: Stakes.

Koivunen, Hannele and Kotro, Tanja (eds) (1999) *Kulttuuriteollisuus* (Cultural Industry), Sitra 214. Helsinki: Sitra.

Koivusalo, Mikko (1995) *Kipinästä tuli syttyy – suomalaisen radiopuhelinteollisuuden kehitys ja tulevaisuuden haasteet* (The Development and Challenges of the Finnish Radio Phone Industry). Espoo: Cetonia Systems.

Kopomaa, Timo (2000) *Kännykkäyhteiskunnan synty.* Helsinki: Gaudeamus.

Korhonen, Teppo (ed.) (1993) *Mitä on suomalaisuus* (What is Finnishness?). Helsinki: Suomen antropologinen seura.

Koski, Heli, Rouvinen, Petri, and Ylä-Anttila, Pekka (2001) *ICT Clusters in Europe: The Great Central Banana and Small Nordic Potato.* Helsinki: Etla, The Research Institute of the Finnish Economy.

# Bibliography

Kuisma, Markku (1996) "Metsässä syntynyt, puusta pudottautunut," in Tarmo Lemola and Raimo Lovio (eds), *Miksi Nokia, Finland* (Why Nokia, Finland?). Porvoo: WSOY.

Kuusi, Pekka (1961) *60-luvun sosiaalipolitiikka* (The Social Policy of the 60s). Porvoo: WSOY.

Laaksonen, Pekka and Mettomäki, Sirkka-Liisa (eds) (1996) *Olkaamme siis suomalaisia* (Let us be Finns), Kalevalaseuran vuosikirja 75–76. Helsinki: Suomalaisen Kirjallisuuden Seura.

Landweber, Lawrence (1987) Letter to Juha Heinänen, November.

Lee, Chong-Moon, Miller, William, Gong Hancock, Marguerite, and Rowen, Henry (2000) *The Silicon Valley Edge: A Habitat for Innovation and Entrepreneurship*. Stanford, CA: Stanford University Press.

Lehtiö, Pekka (1998) *Tietoverkot ja digitaaliset oppimateriaalit, Tieto- ja viestintätekniikka opetuksessa ja oppimisessa* (Networks and Digital Learning Materials), Report 5, Sitra 193. Helsinki: Sitra.

Lehtisalo, Liekki (ed.) (1994) *Sivistys 2017* (Education 2017), Sitra 132. Helsinki: WSOY.

Lehto, Juhani and Blomster, Peter (1999) "1990-luvun alun lama ja sosiaali-ja terveyspalvelupolitiikan suunta" (The Recession of the Early 1990s and the Trend of Social and Health Services Policy), *Yhteiskuntapolitiikka*, 64 (3).

Lehtonen, Tuomas (ed.) (1999) *Europe's Northern Frontier: Perspectives on Finland's Western Identity*. Porvoo: PS-Kustannus.

Leiner, Barry, Cerf, Vinton, Clark, David, Kahn, Robert, Kleinrock, Leonard, Lynch, Daniel, Postel, Jon, Roberts, Lawrence, and Wolff, Stephen, A Brief History of the Internet, Internet Society, 2000, http://www.isoc.org/internet/history/brief.shtml.

Lemola, Tarmo (1996) "Riittääkö kolme miljardia markkaa?" (Is Three Billion Marks Enough?), in Tarmo Lemola and Raimo Lovio (eds), *Miksi Nokia, Finland* (Why Nokia, Finland?). Porvoo: WSOY.

—— (2001) *Tiedettä, teknologiaa ja innovaatioita kansakunnan parhaaksi: Katsaus Suomen tiede- ja teknologiapolitiikan lähihistoriaan* (Science, Technology, and Innovations for the Good of the Nation). Espoo: VTT Teknologian tutkimuksen ryhmän työpaperi 57.

—— and Lovio, Raimo (eds) (1996) *Miksi Nokia, Finland* (Why Nokia, Finland?), Porvoo: WSOY.

Levy, Steven (1984) *Hackers: Heroes of the Computer Revolution*, 2nd edn, 1994. New York: Delta.

Lilius, Reijo (1997) *Suomi tietoyhteiskunnaksi: Kansallisten linjausten arviointi* (Finland into an Information Society: An Evaluation of National Goals), Sitra 159. Helsinki: Sitra.

# Bibliography

—— (1998) *Suomalaisen tietoyhteiskunnan hankkeet ja rakentajat* (The Projects and Builders of the Finnish Information Society), Sitra 167. Helsinki: Sitra.

—— (1999) *Suomalaiset tietoyhteiskuntaprojektit: Kärkihanke-kohtainen tilannearvio* (The Finnish Information Society Projects: An Evaluation of the Spearhead Projects). Helsinki: Sitra.

Linna, Väinö (1969) *The Unknown Soldier*. Porvoo: WSOY.

Loikkanen, Heikki, Rantala, Anssi, and Sullström, Risto (1998) *Regional Income Differences in Finland, 1966–1996*. Helsinki: Valtion taloudellinen tutkimuskeskus (Government Institute for Economic Research).

Lönnrot, Elias (ed.) (1989) *Kalevala*, trans. Keith Bosley. Oxford: Oxford University Press.

Lovio, Raimo (1996) "Yhtymien muodonmuutokset ja liiketoimintojen kiertokulku" (The Transformation of Corporations and the Cycles of Businesses), in Tarmo Lemola and Raimo Tovio (eds), *Miksi Nokia, Finland* (Why Nokia, Finland?). Porvoo: SWOY.

Löytönen, Markku and Kolbe, Laura (eds) (1999) *Suomi: Maa, kansa, kulttuurit* (Finland: The Country, Nation, and Cultures). Helsinki: Suomalaisen Kirjallisuuden Seura.

Lundvall, B-Å. (ed.) (1992) *Natural Systems of Innovation: Towards a Theory of Innovation and Interactive Learning*. London: Pinter.

Mäenpää, Pasi (2000) "Kännykkä ja urbaani elämäntapa," in T. Hoikkala and J. P. Roos (eds), *2000-luvun elämä. Sosiologisia teorioita vuosituhannen vaihteesta*. Helsinki: Gaudeamus.

Mäkinen, Marco (1995) *Nokia saga: kertomus yrityksestä ja ihmisistä jotka muuttivat sen* (Nokia Saga: A Story of the Company and the People who Transformed it). Jyväskylä: Gummerus.

Mäkinen, M., Pajarinen, M., Kivisaari, S., and Kortelainen, S. (1999) *Hyvinvointiklusterin vientimenestys ja teollinen toiminta 1990-luvulla* (The Export Success and Industrial Activity of the Well-being Cluster in the 1990s). Helsinki: Etla Keskusteluaiheita no. 666.

Maliranta, Mika (2001) *Productivity Growth and Micro-level Restructuring: Finnish Experiences during the Turbulent Decades*, discussion paper 757. Helsinki: Etla (http://www.etla.fi/english/research/publications/searchengine/pdf/dp/dp757.pdf).

Michelsen, Karl-Erik (1996) "Kari Kairamon unelma: eurooppalainen Suomi" (Kari Kairamo's Dream: A European Finland), in Tarmo Lemola and Raimo Lovio (eds), *Miksi Nokia, Finland* (Why Nokia, Finland?). Porvoo: WSOY.

# Bibliography

Miettinen, Reijo, Lehenkari, Janne, Hasu, Mervi, and Hyvönen, Jukka (1999) *Osaaminen ja uuden luominen innovaatioverkoissa* (Innovation Networks as a Source of New Knowledge and Products), Sitra 226. Helsinki: Taloustieto.

Ministry of Education (1995) *Koulutuksen ja tutkimuksen tietostrategia* (The Information Strategy for Education and Research), Helsinki, http://www.miniedu.fi/tietostrategia/tietostrategia.html.

—— (1996) *Kulttuurinen tietoyhteiskunta: Strategiset perusteet ja lähtökohdat opetusministeriön toimintaohjelmalle vuosiksi 1997–2000*. Helsinki.

—— (1997) *Opetusministeriön tietostrategioiden tilanne* (The State of Implementation of the Ministry's Educational Strategies), September, Helsinki, www.minedu.fi/julkaisut/julkaisusarjat/ tietostr.html.

—— (1999*a*) *Koulutuksen ja tutkimuksen tietostrategia 2000–2004* (Education, Training, and Research in the Information Society: A National Strategy for 2000–2004). Helsinki.

—— (1999*b*) *Koulutuksen ja tutkimuksen tietostrategia: Hankesuunnitelmat* (Education, Training, and Research in the Information Society: The Project Plans), Helsinki, http://www. minedu.fi/julkaisut/pdf/ tietostrategia/hankesuunnitelmat.pdf.

—— (1999*c*) *Kulttuuriteollisuustyöryhmän loppuraportti*. Helsinki.

—— (2001) *Koulutuksen ja tutkimuksen tietostrategian 2000–2004 toimeenpanosuunnitelma* (Education, Training, and Research in the Information Society: The Implementation Plan). Helsinki.

Ministry of Education Information Skills Working Group (2000) *Suomi (o)saa lukea* (Finnish Net Literacy). Helsinki: Ministry of Education.

Ministry of Education Working Group for Content Production (2001) *Sisältötuotanto -työryhmän väliraportti*. Helsinki.

Ministry of Finance (1995) *Suomi tietoyhteiskunnaksi: Kansalliset linjaukset* (Finland's Way to the Information Society: The National Strategy). Helsinki.

—— (1996) *Finland's Way to the Information Society: The National Strategy and its Implementation*. Helsinki.

Ministry of Social Affairs and Health (1996) *Sosiaali- ja terveydenhuollon tietoteknologian hyödyntämisstrategia* (The Social and Health Service Strategy for the Utilization of ICT), työryhmämuistioita, 27. Helsinki.

—— (1998*a*) *Sosiaali- ja terveydenhuollon tietoteknologian hyödyntäminen 1: Saumaton hoito- ja palveluketju* (The Social and Health Service Strategy for the Utilization of ICT: The Seamless Care and Service Chain). Helsinki.

# Bibliography

—— (1998b) *Sosiaali- ja terveydenhuollon tietoteknologian hyödyntäminen 2: Tietosuoja ja tietoturva* (The Social and Health Service Strategy for the Utilization of ICT: Privacy and Data Security). Helsinki.

—— (1998c) *Sosiaali- ja terveydenhuollon tietoteknologian hyödyntäminen 2 Liite: Tietoturvateknologian yleiskatsaus* (The Social and Health Service Strategy for the Utilization of ICT: An Overview of the Data Security Technology). Helsinki.

—— (2001) *Tietoteknologia, saumattomuus, asiakaslähtöisyys: Tietoteknologia sosiaali- ja terveydenhuollon palvelujärjestelmässä – Hyväksi arvioitujen toiminnallisten ja teknisten ratkaisujen käyttöönotto ja juurruttamissuunnitelma vuosille 2001–2003* (Information Technology, Seamlessness, and Customer-centeredness). Helsinki: Stakes.

Ministry of Transportation and Communications (2001) *Tekstiviestimarkkinat 1999–2002*. Helsinki: Edita.

Mitchell, William J. (1999) *E-topia: "Urban Life, Jim – But Not as We Know It."* Cambridge, MA: MIT Press.

Moisala, U.E., Rahko, Kauko, and Turpeinen, Oiva (1977) *Puhelin ja puhelinlaitokset Suomessa 1877–1977* (The History of Telephone and Telephone Cooperatives in Finland 1877–1977). Turku: Puhelinlaitosten Liitto.

Moody, Glyn (2001) *Rebel Code: Inside Linux and the Open Source Revolution*. Cambridge, MA: Perseus.

Nasdaq (2001) "Market Statistics 1971–2001," http://www.marketdata. nasdaq.com/mr4b.html.

Nelson, R. (ed.) (1993) *National Innovation Systems: A Comparative Study*. Oxford: Oxford University Press.

Netcraft (2001) *SSL Server Survey*, January, http://www.netcraft.com/ surveys/analysis/https/2001/Jan/Cmatch/strength.html.

Nevalainen, Risto (1999) *Suomi tietoyhteiskunnaksi – eespäin tiedon poluilla ja valtateillä: Tietoyhteiskuntatoiminnan lyhyt historia*. Helsinki: Sitra (www.sitra.fi/tietoyhteiskunta/suomi/nevalaisenhistoria.html).

Nevgi, Anne (2000) *Koulutuksen ja tutkimuksen tietostrategian 1995–99 vaikuttavuuden arviointi* (An Evaluation of the Impact of the Information Strategy for Education and Research 1995–99). Helsinki: Parliament of Finland Committee for the Future and Sitra (www.minedu.fi/julkaisut/julkaisusarjat/tietostr.html).

Nokia (2000a) *Business Review 2000*. Helsinki: Nokia.

—— (2000b) *Financial Statements 2000*. Helsinki: Nokia.

—— (2000c) *Nokia Research Center*. Helsinki: Nokia.

# Bibliography

OECD (Organization for Economic Co-operation and Development) (1999) *Science, Technology and Industry Scoreboard 1999: Benchmarking Knowledge-based Economies.* Paris: OECD.

—— (2000) *Measuring the ICT Sector.* Paris: OECD.

—— (2001a) *Communications Outlook 2001.* Paris: OECD.

—— (2001b) *Standardized Unemployment Rates,* July. Paris: OECD (http://www.oecd.org/media/new-numbers/sur/sur01-07a.pdf).

—— (2001c) *Knowledge and Skills for Life: First Results from PISA 2000.* Paris: OECD.

Ohinmaa, Arto, Pietilä, Marjukka, and Valtonen, Hannu (1999) *Hyvinvointiklusterin väliraportointi: Hyvä asiakkuus* (A Preliminary Report on the Well-being Cluster), Stakes Aiheita 12. Helsinki: Stakes.

Oikarinen, Jarkko (1993) "Early IRC History", www.irc.org/history_docs/jarkko.html.

Oksa, Jukka and Turunen, Jarno (2000a) *Paikallinen kansalaisverkko: Oppivan Ylä-Karjalan arviointitutkimus,* Karelian Institute working papers no. 5/2000. Joensuu: University of Joensuu.

—— —— (2000b) *Local Community Net: Evaluation Study of the Learning Upper Karelia Project,* Karelian Institute working papers no. 5/2000. Joensuu: University of Joensuu.

OpenSSH (2001) "OpenSSH", http://www.openssh.com/history.html.

Otala, Matti (2001) *Uskalla olla viisas* (Dare to be Wise). Helsinki: Ajatus.

Paaso, Pia (1999) *Hyvinvointia tietoteknologiahankkeilla: Valtakunnallinen sosiaali- ja terveydenhuollon hankekartoitus.* Helsinki: Sosiaali- ja terveysministeriö.

Paavolainen, Jaakko (1966) *Poliittiset väkivaltaisuudet Suomessa 1917–1918, I Punainen terrori* (The Political Violence in Finland 1917–1918: The Red Terror). Helsinki: Tammi.

—— (1967) *Poliittiset väkivaltaisuudet Suomessa 1917–1918, II Valkoinen terrori* (The Political Violence in Finland 1917–1918: The White Terror). Helsinki: Tammi.

—— (1971) *Poliittiset väkivaltaisuudet Suomessa 1917–1918, III Vankileirit Suomessa 1918* (The Political Violence in Finland 1917–1918: The Prison Camps in Finland in 1918). Helsinki: Tammi.

Paija, Laura (2000) *ICT Cluster: The Engine of Knowledge-driven Growth in Finland,* ETLA discussion papers 733. Helsinki: Etla.

—— (ed.) (2001) *Finnish ICT Cluster in the Global Digital Economy.* Helsinki: Etla.

# Bibliography

Palmberg, Christopher, Niininen, Petri, Toivanen, Hannes, and Wahlberg, Tanja (2000) *Industrial Innovation in Finland: First Results of the Sfinno-Project*, 2000, working papers no. 47/00. Espoo: VTT.

Pantzar, Mika and Ainamo, Antti (2001) "Nokia: The Surprising Success of Textbook Wisdom", unpublished manuscript.

Parliament of Finland Committee for the Future (1998a) "Tieto- ja viestintätekniikka opetuksessa ja oppimisessa, esiraportti" (ICT in Teaching and Learning: A Preliminary Report), in Matti Sinko and Erno Lehtinen (eds.), *Technology Assessment 2*. Helsinki.

——— (1998b) *Report on the Government's Report on the Future*. Helsinki.

——— (1999a) "Tieto- ja viestintätekniikka opetuksessa ja oppimisessa" (ICT in Teaching and Learning), in Matti Sinko and Erno Lehtinen (eds.), *Technology Assessment 4*. Helsinki (http://www.eduskunta.fi/fakta/vk/tuv/tekjaosto/msinko.htm).

——— (1999b) "Esiselvitys geronteknologiasta: Ikääntyvä väestö ja teknologian mahdollisuudet" (A Preliminary Report on Gerontechnology), in Juha Kaakinen and Sinikka Törmä, *Technology Assessment 5*. Helsinki (http://www. eduskunta.fi/fakta/vk/tuv/tekjaosto/geron.pdf).

Pentikäinen, Tuomo (2000) *Economic Evaluation of the Finnish Cluster Programmes*, VTT Group for Technology Studies, working paper no. 50. Espoo: VTT.

Pine, Joseph and Gilmore, James (1999) *The Experience Economy: Work is Theatre and Every Business a Stage*. Cambridge, MA: Harvard Business School Press.

Porter, M. (1990) *The Competitive Advantage of Nations*. New York: The Free Press.

Prihti, Aatto, Georghiou, Luke, Helander, Elisabeth, Juusela, Jyrki, Meyer-Krahmer, Frieder, Roslin, Bertil, Santamäki-Vuori, Tuire, and Gröhn, Mirja (2000) *Assessment of the Additional Appropriation for Research*. Helsinki: Hakapaino.

Pulkkinen, Matti (1996) "Miten jättiläisiä horjutetaan?" (How to Sway Giants?) in Tarmo Lemola and Raimo Lovio (eds), *Miksi Nokia, Finland* (Why Konia, Finland?). Porvoo: WSOY.

——— (1997) *The Breakthrough of Nokia Mobile Phones*, Acta Universitatis Oeconomicae Helsingiensis A 122. Helsinki: Helsinki School of Economics and Business Administration.

Putnam, Robert (1995) "Bowling Alone: America's Declining Social Capital," *Journal of Democracy*, 6 (1).

# Bibliography

Quittner, Joshua (1994) "Anonymously Yours – An Interview with Johan Helsingius", *Wired*, 2 June, http://www.wired.com/wired/2.06/departments/electrosphere/anonymous.1.html.

Raymond, Eric (ed.) (2001) *The Jargon File*, http://www.tuxedo.org/~esr/jargon.

Riihelä, Marja and Sullström, Risto (2001) *Tuloerot ja eriarvoisuus suuralueilla pitkällä aikavälillä 1971–1998 ja erityisesti 1990-luvulla* (Income Differences and Inequality by Regions in the Long Run 1971–1998 and Especially in the 1990s). Helsinki: Government Institute for Economic Research.

Riihelä, Marja, Sullström, Risto, Suoniemi, Ilpo, and Tuomala, Matti (2001) "Income Inequality in Finland during the 1990s," in Kalela Jorma *et al.* (eds), *Down from the Heavens, Up from the Ashes: The Finnish Economic Crisis of the 1990s in the Light of Economic and Social Research*. Helsinki: Valtion taloudellinen tutkimuskeskus (Government Institute for Economic Research).

Riihinen, Olavi (ed.) (1992) *Sosiaalipolitiikka 2017: Näkökulmia suomalaisen yhteiskunnan kehitykseen ja tulevaisuuteen* (Social Policy 2017), Sitra 123. Porvoo: WSOY.

Ritakallio, Veli-Matti (2001) "Multidimensional Poverty in the Aftermath of the Recession: Finland in 1995 and 2000," in Jarma Kalela *et al.* (eds), *Down from the Heavens, Up from the Ashes: The Finnish Economic Crisis of the 1990s in the Light of Economic and Social Research*. Helsinki: Valtion taloudellinen tutkimuskeskus (Government Institute for Economic Research).

Rouvinen, P., Saranummi, N., and Lammi, M. (eds) (1995) *Terveydenhuolto versoo teollisuutta: Hyvinvointivaltion kilpailukyky* (Health Care as an Industry: The Competitiveness of the Welfare State). Etla, series B 109. Helsinki: Taloustieto.

Ruokanen, Tapani and Nurmio, Aarne (eds) (1995) *Suomi ja mahdolliset maailmat* (Finland and the Possible Worlds), Sitra 146. Juva: WSOY.

Saarelainen, Anu (ed.) (2000) *Kyläteiltä tiedon valtateille: Oppiva Ylä-Karjala tienraivaajana* (From the Village Paths to the Information Super Highways: The Upper Karelia Learning Project as a Pioneer Project), Sitra 235. Kuopio: Kevama Graf.

Saari, Matti (2000) *Kari Kairamo: Kohtalona Nokia* (Kari Kairamo: Nokia as the Fate). Jyväskylä: Gummerus.

Salminen, Harri (1999) "History of the Internet", http://www.funet.fi/index/FUNET/history/internet/en/.

# Bibliography

Saranummi, Niilo (1999) "Well-being Cluster", http://www.vtt.fi/tte/samba/project/well-being/.

Saxenian, Annalee (1994) *Regional Advantage: Culture and Competition in Silicon Valley and Route 128.* Cambridge, MA: Harvard University Press.

—— (1999) *Silicon Valley's New Immigrant Entrepreneurs.* San Francisco: Public Policy Institute of California.

Schienstock, Gerd and Hämäläinen, T. (2001) *Transformation of the Finnish Innovation System: A Network Approach.* Helsinki: Sitra.

—— and Kuusi, Osmo (eds) (1999) *Transformation Towards a Learning Economy: The Challenge for the Finnish Innovation System,* Sitra 213. Helsinki: Sitra.

Science and Technology Policy Council of Finland (1987) *Review 1987.* Helsinki.

—— (1990) *Review 1990: Guidelines for Science and Technology Policy.* Helsinki.

—— (1993) *Towards an Innovative Society: A Development Strategy for Finland.* Helsinki.

—— (1996a) *Finland: A Knowledge-based Society.* Helsinki: Edita.

—— (1996b) *Tutkimusra-hoituksen lisäyksen käyttösuunnitelma 1997–1999, tutkimuspanos vuonna 2000* (A Plan for the Use of the Additional Appropriation for Research 1997–1999). Helsinki.

—— (2000) *Review 2000: The Challenge of Knowledge and Know-how.* Helsinki: Edita.

Siisiäinen, Martti (1999) "Voluntary Associations and Social Capital in Finland," in Jan W. van Deth, Marco Maraffi, Ken Newton and Paul F. Whiteley (eds), *Social Capital and European Democracy.* London: Routledge.

Siltala, Juha (1985) *Lapuanliike ja kyyditykset 1930* (The Lapua Movement and Beatings 1930). Helsinki: Otava.

Simpura, Jussi, Blomster, Peter, Heikkilä, Matti, Häkkinen, Unto, Kautto, Mikko, Keskimäki, Ilmo, Lehto, Juhani, Rastas, Merja, Rissanen, Pekka, and Valtonen, Hannu (2001) "The Survival of the Finnish Health and Welfare System during the Economic Depression of the 1990s", forthcoming in J. Kiander *et al.* (eds), *Down from the Heavens, Up from the Ashes: The Finnish Economic Recession in the 1990s.*

Singapore Department of Statistics (2001) *Singapore Census of Population, 2000,* http://www.singstat.gov.sg/C2000/adr-hhinc.pdf.

Singleton Frederick (1989) *A Short History of Finland.* New York: Cambridge University Press.

# Bibliography

Sinko, Matti and Lehtinen, Erno (1999) *The Challenges of ICT in Finnish Education*, Sitra 227. Juva: WSOY.

Sitra (1998) *Elämänlaatu, osaaminen ja kilpailukyky: Tietoyhteiskunnan strategisen kehittämisen lähtökohdat ja päämäärät* (Quality of Life, Knowledge and Competitiveness: Premises and Objective for Strategic Development of the Finnish Information Society), Sitra 206. Helsinki: Sitra.

Sonkin, Leif, Petäkoski-Hult, Tuula, Ronka, Kimmo, and Södergård, Hans (1999) *Seniori 2000: Ikääntyvä Suomi uudelle vuosituhannelle* (Senior 2000: The Aging Finland in a New Millennium), Sitra 233. Helsinki: Taloustieto.

Stakes (1997) *Oulun seudun hyvinvoinklusteri* (The Oulu Region Well-being Cluster).

Stallman, Richard (1985) "The GNU Manifesto", www.gnu.org/gnu/manifesto.html, 1993.

—— (1999) "The GNU Operating System and the Free Software Movement" in Chris DiBona, Sam Ockham, and Mark Stone (eds), *Open Sources: Voices from the Open Source Revolution*. Sebastopol, CA: O'Reilly (www.oreilly.com/catalog/opensources/book/stallman.html and www.gnu.org/gnu/thegnuproject).

Statistics Finland (2000) *Statistical Yearbook of Finland 2000*. Helsinki: Statistics Finland.

Steinbock, Dan (2000*a*) *Finland's Wireless Valley: From Industrial Policies Toward Cluster Strategies*, Ministry of Transport and Communications 36/2000. Helsinki: Edita.

—— (2000*b*) *Sonera's Evolution*. Helsinki: Sonera.

—— (2001) *The Nokia Revolution: The Story of an Extraordinary Company that Transformed an Industry*. New York: Amacom.

Taipale, Vappu (1994) "Hyvinvointiklusteriin käsiksi" (Hands on the Well-being Cluster), *Dialogi*, 8.

Technology Committee (1982) *The Report of the Finnish Technology Committee*. Helsinki: Publication of the Office of the Prime Minister.

Titmuss, Richard (1968) *Commitment to Welfare*. London: Allen and Unwin.

—— (1974) *Social Policy: An Introduction*. London: Allen and Unwin.

Toivola, Keijo (1992) *Poimintoja teletoimen historiasta* (Selections from the History of Telecommunications Business). Helsinki: Tele.

Torvalds, Linus (1991*a*) "What Would You Like to See Most in Minix?," a message to comp.os.minix, August 25.

—— (1991*b*) "Free Minix-like Kernel Source for 386-AT," a message to comp.os.minix, October 5.

—— (1992*a*) "Re: Writing an OS," a message to linux-activists@bloompicayune.mit.edu, May 5.

—— (1992*b*) "Birthday," a message to linux-activists@bloom-picayune. mit.edu, July 31.

—— with David Diamond) (2001) *Just for Fun: The Story of an Accidental Revolutionary.* New York: HarperBusiness.

Townsend, Anthony (2000) *Life in the Real-time City: Mobile Telephones and Urban Metabolism.* New York: New York University Press.

Tuomi, Ilkka (1999) *Corporate Knowledge: Theory and Practice of Intelligent Organizations.* Helsinki: Metaxis.

Turpeinen, Oiva (1996*a*) *Yhdistämme: 200 vuotta historiaa – haasteena tulevaisuus Lennätinlaitoksesta Telecom Finland Oy:ksi* (Connecting: 200 Years of History – the Future as the Challenge. From a Telegraph Company to Telecom Finland, Inc.). Helsinki: Edita. (An abridged version has been published as *Telecommunications since 1796.*)

—— (1996*b*) *Malliksi maailmalle: Suomen televiestinnän monopolien murtuminen 1977–96* (Setting an Example to the World: The Breaking of the Finnish Telecommunications Monopolies 1977–96). Salpausselkä: Finnet-liitto.

UNDP (United Nations Development Programme) (1999) *Human Development Report 1999.* Oxford: Oxford University Press.

—— (2000) *Human Development Report 2000.* Oxford: Oxford University Press.

—— (2001) *Human Development Report 2001.* Oxford: Oxford University Press.

United Nations Population Fund (2000) *The State of the World Population 2000.* New York: UNFPA.

United States Bureau of Justice Statistics (1992) *Sourcebook of Criminal Justice Statistics.* Washington, DC: US Department of Justice.

United States Census Bureau (1999) *Money Income in the United States 1998.* Washington, DC: United States Census Bureau.

Väänänen, Teemu (1996) "Yhtymäjohtamisen ja kansallisen kehikon muutos" (The Change in Corporate Management and the National Framework), in Tarmo Lemola and Raimo Lovio (eds), *Miksi Nokia, Finland* (Why Nokia, Finland?). Porvoo: WSOY.

Vartia, Pentti and Ylä-Anttila, Pekka (1992) *Kansantalous 2017* (The National Economy 2017), Sitra 12. Helsinki: Sitra.

Viteli, Jarmo (ed.) (1998) *Esimerkkejä ja kokemuksia korkeakoulumaailmasta* (Examples and Experiences from the Universities), Ticto- ja viestintätekniikka opetuksessa ja oppimisessa report 2, Sitra 190. Helsinki: Sitra.

Viteli, Jarmo, Collan, Seppo, Kauppi, Antti, Niemi, Hannele, and Vainio, Leena (eds) (1998) *Yliopistojen ja ammattikorkeakoulujen tilanne ja tulevaisuudennäkymät* (The State and Future Prospects of the Universities

# Bibliography

and Polytechnics), Tieto- ja viestintätekniikka opetuksessa ja oppimisessa report 1, Sitra 189. Helsinki: Sitra.

Vuori, Synnöve and Vuorinen, Pentti (eds) (1994) *Explaining Technical Change in a Small Country: The Finnish National Innovation System.* Heidelberg/Helsinki: Physica-Verlag/Etla.

Vuorinen, Pentti, Tikka, Tiina, and Lovio, Raimo (1989) *Suomen Teknologiakeskukset* (Finnish Technology Parks). Helsinki: Vapk.

Weber, Max (1904–5) *The Protestant Ethic and the Spirit of Capitalism*, trans. Talcott Parsons. London: Routledge, 1997.

WEF (World Economic Forum) (2000) *The Global Competitiveness Report 2000.* New York: Oxford University Press.

Wheeler, James, Aoyama, Yuko, and Warf, Barney (eds) (2000) *Cities in the Telecommunications Age: The Fracturing of Geographies.* London: Routledge.

Wilensky, Harold and Lebeaux, Charles (1958) *Industrial Society and Social Welfare.* New York: Russell Sage Foundation.

World Bank (2000) *World Development Report 2000/2001: Attacking Poverty.* Oxford: Oxford University Press.

Ylikangas, Heikki (1993*a*) *Tie Tampereelle 1918: Dokumentoitu kuvaus Tampereen antautumiseen johtaneista sotatapahtumista Suomen sisällissodassa* (The Way to Tampere 1918: A Documented Description of the War Events that Led to Tampere's Surrender in the Finnish Civil War). Porvoo: WSOY.

—— (ed.) (1993*b*) *Vaikea totuus: Vuosi 1918 ja kansallinen tiede* (The Difficult Truth: The Year 1918 and National Science). Helsinki: Suomalaisen kirjallisuuden seura.

Zook, Matthew (2000) "The Web of Production: The Economic Geography of Commercial Internet Content Production in the United States," *Environment and Planning*, 32.

—— (2001) "Old Hierarchies or New Networks of Centrality?: The Global Geography of the Internet Content Market," *American Behavioral Scientist*, 44 (10).

# Index

# Index

# Index

# Index